Supervision and Team Support

SOCIAL WORK PRACTICE IN FSU

Other books in this series:

1. *Direct Work with Families*
   edited by J. Miller and T. Cook

2. *Direct Work with Children*
   edited by S. Martel

SOCIAL WORK PRACTICE IN FSU

3 Supervision and Team Support

edited by

Sheila Martel

Published for the Family Service Units by the
BEDFORD SQUARE PRESS   NCVO

First published 1981 by the
Bedford Square Press of the
National Council for Voluntary Organisations
26 Bedford Square London WC1B 3HU

© Family Service Units 1981

ISBN 0 7199 1066 8

Printed in England by H. Ling Ltd, The Dorset Press, Dorchester, Dorset

Contents

Acknowledgements

None of the books in this series on social work practice in Family Service Units could have been produced without an enormous amount of help from a wide range of people far too numerous to list individually. We are very grateful to Unit staff and committees who enabled the contributors to find the time and space to write up their work. The ideas and comments that came from colleagues, relatives and friends were all much appreciated. Secretarial staff in Units and outside have been very patient with innumerable drafts and strange handwriting: they are owed many thanks. Finally we acknowledge that while authors are named, family names have been changed for anonymity, yet the part they play goes beyond that of 'client'. We thank them for their contribution and their courage.

Notes on Contributors

Sheila Martel has been Assistant Director of Family Service Units since 1972, following experience as Children's Officer in Guernsey, Adoptions Officer and Training Officer with Surrey Children's Department.

Gemma Blech was a trained nurse and midwife before undertaking social work training at the London School of Economics. She worked for two years in an Inner London Social Services Department before becoming Unit Organiser of the Queens Park Unit in 1975.

David Horn worked as a Child Care Officer before training in social work at Keele University. He was a social worker, a community worker, and community work adviser with Nottinghamshire Social Services Department before becoming Unit Organiser of the East Birmingham Unit from 1976 to 1980.

Rosemary Clews taught sociology in a College of Further Education before becoming a social worker in 1975. She worked for the Child Guidance Service in Birmingham until joining FSU in 1978.

Janet West has been Student Training Organiser at the Leicester Unit since 1976. She trained as a mature probation student, and worked for ten years as a Probation Officer in Leicestershire.

Pam Donnellan joined the Leicester Unit as Groupworker in 1978, following experience in residential and field social work, and four years as a Probation Officer in Surrey.

Pam Wood was appointed as Social Worker/Volunteer Organiser at the Leicester Unit in 1978, following experience as a social worker with Barnado's and Wolverhampton Social Services Department.

Introduction

This is the third book in a series about social work practice in Family Service Units. In the first of these, [1] the theoretical bases for practice are described, with an outline of the history and development of the agency, followed by examples of individual pieces of work. The second book [2] discusses the content and process of work where there is particular concern about the care and development of children. In this third book, the supervision and team support essential for all the Units' work is considered.

When working with families who experience a number of entrenched and interrelated difficulties, it is easy for the social workers to become enmeshed in the chaos that the families present, and to lose direction and purpose in their work. When the high stress of family violence is added, workers can become caught in anxiety which is reinforced by pressure from other agencies, the media and the public. For a 'burnt-out' social worker, escape may lie in leaving the profession, or in climbing the promotional ladder into management and administration.

In FSU, supervision and team support have always been given a high priority – indeed they are seen as essential prerequisites for carrying out effective work. It is perhaps important to distinguish what is meant by these terms, as they are used very differently in other contexts.

Supervision in social work should not be the mere checking of a person's work task which may be appropriate in an industrial setting, though it can be the case that in some voluntary and statutory agencies social workers receive little more than this. Supervision should include elements of training in theory and task-related skills, professional development, focused discussion of aims, evaluation of the work undertaken and workload management. It should be regular, uninterrupted and structured, yet there are times when the supervisor needs to be available to the worker between the regular supervision sessions, particularly for newly appointed staff, or where serious crises arise. The supervisor needs to acquire skills in addition to the skills and experience gained as a social worker. All too often it is assumed that because a person has professional social work skills and experience, the step to becoming a good supervisor is automatic, without recognising the different skills that are involved. The aim of supervision should not be only to ensure that the social worker is carrying out his task within the policies and to the standard required by the agency. More important is the aim of enabling the worker to develop his abilities to the maximum, in providing the best possible service to clients, and to increase his own survival chances and job satisfaction.

The above statements would appear to place a heavy responsibility on the individual supervisor, and this is appropriate. Nevertheless, it is limited if it is not combined with a team structure which is both stimulating and supportive. The opportunities for social workers to learn from each other are greatly enhanced in a team where active discussion and co-operation are encouraged, and in work with severely disadvantaged families and communities good teamwork is essential. In FSU, active participation of all staff in policy decision making and professional practice issues has always been recognised as important. This participation is real and effective, and not the 'tokenism' which can exist in more rigidly hierarchical organisations. It does, of course, carry with it the dangers of discussion and consultation becoming too time consuming; a continuing tension exists to achieve a healthy balance between democratic discussion and efficient decision making.

In the two earlier books in this series [1, 2], it can be seen that the local autonomy of units, and the aim of creating innovative services, leads to considerable variation between the services and methods used in Units, within the overall aims of the organisation as a whole. That variation is also reflected in this book. The papers come from three Units, Queens Park, East Birmingham and Leicester, and in each case the supervision and team structures have been developed in the context of each Unit's approach to its work. The common threads which bind them, in addition to the shared organisational aims and ethos, are the emphasis on team building and the high priority which is given to constructive and creative supervision of all involved in the work, be they social workers, students, administrative staff or volunteers.

The first chapter is written by Gemma Blech, Unit Organiser of the Queens Park Unit. The Unit was established in 1973 on the edge of a heavily populated Victorian housing estate, with its premises in the busy main shopping street. The base of the Unit's work is strongly influenced by psychoanalytical theory. This theoretical base informs the use of a range of different work methods, such as structural family therapy, marital therapy, group relations or play therapy, but the psychodynamic approach ensures that work plans are informed by, and take account of, the basic theories of the unconscious in family dynamics. Action research undertaken by the

Institute of Marital Studies [3] has shown that for effective psychodynamic work to take place with couples experiencing marital problems, the structure of the agency must be geared to the work methods being used if the aims of the work are not to be undermined. This has certainly been our experience. For this reason the commitment of the Unit team to the work approach is reinforced by appointing staff who share a commitment to psychodynamic work. Applicants are given ample opportunity to test out both the style of the group and that of the Unit Organiser/supervisor before appointment.

Chapter 2 is written by David Horn and Rosemary Clews, Unit Organiser and social worker at the East Birmingham Unit. The Unit was established early in FSU's history, and therefore has been through many stages in the development of social work theory and practice. It is one of the larger units, with nine social workers and a student training unit. For two years it also ran a community work project from premises in an area undergoing demolition. The chapter describes the changes that took place in the work and team structure of the Unit as the full implications of systems theory and the unitary approach were assimilated.

The final three chapters are written by members of the Leciester Unit, another large and long established Unit. The main Unit, near the centre of the city, houses the caseworkers, a student training unit, groupwork rooms and the administrative staff. A neighbourhood centre and a parent and child centre on an estate on the outskirts of the city provide community work, advice services and a general resource for mothers and young children. During the last three years, the Unit has developed a family work method based on general systems theory. The method concentrates on the problems actually experienced by families, be they external stress linked to poverty, housing, schools etc., or internal stress caused by behavioural or control problems exhibited by children, or marital difficulties. In particular the Unit looks at the consequences indicated by general systems theory, in relation to boundaries, hierarchies, sequences and causality, to which are added elements of communication and learning theory. Intervention is aimed at changing the patterns of exchange, using techniques of family therapy, [4] problem solving, [5] social skills learning [6] and behaviour modification. The chapters on student supervision, groupwork supervision and the support and supervision of volunteers are therefore seen in the context of the aims and work of the Unit as a whole.

In describing three units so briefly, it is easy to distort by oversimplification, and to emphasise the differences between them, and between them and other units, rather than the common elements they share. There is considerable exchange of ideas between units, and most of the theories and practice methods described have influenced all units to some extent. Balances and emphases may differ, as each unit team works together to develop and improve its own package of theory, method and services.

In all three books in this series it has been our aim to concentrate on the process and content of the work, so that others may take and use where appropriate in their own work the practice we have described. We firmly believe that for high standards of effective social work practice to be developed, supervision and the development of team support structures need to be given high priority. The following chapters therefore include a number of practical examples of the content of supervision, and the processes which enhance teamwork. It is our hope that those who read this book will be able to take and use some of the methods and techniques we describe, to the benefit of their own practice.

References

1. J. Miller and T. Cook (eds.), *Direct Work with Families*. Bedford Square Press, 1981.

2. S. Martel (ed.), *Direct Work with Children*. Bedford Square Press, 1981.

3. J. Mattinson and I. Sinclair, *Mate and Stalemate*. Blackwell, 1979.

4. S. Walrond Skinner and R. Skynner, *Family Therapy*. Routledge and Kegan Paul, 1976.

5. J. Haley, *Problem Solving Therapy*. Jossey-Bass, 1978.

6. P. Priestley, J. McGuire et al., *Social Skills and Personal Problem Solving*. Tavistock, 1978.

1. How to prevent 'Burn Out' of Social Workers

A Psychodynamic perspective of Supervision with Special Reference to Work with Abusing and Neglectful Families

Gemma Blech

Introduction

I consider supervision to be the key to good social work practice and if good practice can be achieved then job satisfaction and low staff turnover will follow. Good practice should also mean improved client well-being. I believe that supervision should be available in all areas of social work when social workers are coming face to face with the emotional and material ills and pains of our society. For the purpose of this paper I shall focus on the individual supervision of social workers who are working with severely disorganised families, most of whom if not actually physically abusing their children are depriving and neglecting them to such an extent that the children are showing 'problems' in the present, and are likely to have few resources on which to build their own families in the future.

Supervision is primarily about work with staff who are working with families and individuals in distress. It is also about a relationship between supervisor and worker, both of whom have agreed to work together; and in the case of FSU, have both chosen to work in a relatively specialised field of social work.

The key to effective supervision is to recognise that there is a relationship between both the social worker and his client, and that same worker and his supervisor. Janet Mattinson writes:

> One of the main attributes of an effective supervisor over and above the possession of a certain amount of skill in the subject or craft which is being taught, is the ability to know about, tolerate and handle three-person relationships. [1]

Whenever a member of staff comes to supervision it needs to be remembered that the worker, the client and I, the supervisor, are in the room.

Because we live in a time of financial stringency and economic difficulties, social workers no less than any others in the helping professions have to prove their worth. Some would question the need for social workers as a body and many social workers have left the profession disillusioned and disenchanted. I do not promote my model of supervision as a solution for all our ills but I do offer a considered view of what I hold to be an essential ingredient for good practice. If good practice can be achieved there will be less disenchantment.

Theoretical Framework

My approach to supervision and to casework is psychodynamic and I draw on a wide range of insights from psychoanalytic literature. Most of us have an eclectic view of social work based on a pragmatism that suits our individual tastes and personality. However, my central emphasis is that supervision is designed to enable workers to engage in a therapeutic relationship with their clients and thus to ensure the highest possible standard of service to them. Sally Hornby wrote in her seminal discussion paper of 1973: [2]

> All work with clients in the helping professions is carried out within the context of a relationship between worker and client. In this the worker should have a psychodynamic approach, which implies recognition of the psychological forces motivating human behaviour and of the importance of feelings in the client's life and in the worker/client relationship.

Supervision should enable this work to take place to maximum effect.

In addition to the psychoanalytic writings of Freud, Jung and Klein, I am indebted to the thinking and writings of many of the current practitioners of social work. I have already quoted Hornby and Mattinson and I would also acknowledge my gratitude to J. Knight, M. Mercer and J. Temperley. They are all practitioners who add a creative dimension to the whole field of social work supervision. I also acknowledge writers and teachers in the whole area of systems theory. From systems theory we learn the importance of boundaries, lines of responsibility, an understanding of bureaucracy, roles and leadership. None of these avenues can be ignored when a supervisor is presented with case material which may require urgent and far-reaching action.

The emphasis of this paper will be on the dynamics operating between individuals, so that with greater understanding social workers may engage in the task of helping to free their clients from some of their painful and destructive situations. Our practice at Queens Park FSU is to have individual supervision for all staff members but some work is supervised in groups. Group supervision is more appropriate when staff are working in pairs in a family, in a group, or in a specialised field of work (e.g. play therapy; family therapy). Our experience would suggest that the more creative, effective and freeing individual supervision can become the more use can be made of group supervision. So this paper concentrates on the content of supervision between one worker and his supervisor. It will only include an understanding of family dynamics when this is crucial to a deeper understanding of the supervisory relationship.

A Definition of Supervision

I share the following definition of social work supervision with all staff on their appointment and would hope that the whole Unit team would continue to discuss and restate the implications of such a definition:

> Supervision is a safe space where the worker together with his supervisor examines the dynamics of the family and its relationship with and within the community; he can examine his own relationship with and feelings about the family and can use this information to determine the nature of presenting problems, areas of work and methods of work and future goals for that family. The interactive process between the supervisor and worker can often be a useful tool in this task.

If the worker is to use supervision time to examine his work in such depth it is imperative that the supervisor recognises the cost and commitment of such a process. Supervision time should be mutually agreed upon and uninterrupted. The supervisor should examine her own skills and be honest enough to admit her own difficulties. She may well need her own 'safe space' to discover her own blind-spots and stretch her understanding.

Responsibility in Supervision

In addition to the 'safe space' concept of supervision the aim of which is to enable creative work to go on, a word needs to be said about responsibility in supervision. In 1976 I wrote a paper [3] suggesting that supervision had two basic components; first that of responsibility and accountability and secondly, that of enabling the social worker to do creative work with the family or individual. The aim of this present paper is to further the discussion of *how* supervision is used to enable better social work practice.

But first a word about responsibility and accountability. I believe no worker, no matter what the level of expertise or experience, should be expected to take decisions alone which affect the life-style of a family. The decision to remove a child from home, return him home or place him in a boarding school is a fundamental change in the life and expectations both of the child and his family and should only be made in discussion with another person. Similarly the decision not to remove a child who is 'at risk' should not be made without proper consultation. The supervisor's role is to ensure that the procedures and people involved in this decision-making process are known to the worker. Decisions such as those described can often be made in principle within supervision. In supervision the needs, dynamics and problems of the family will have been properly understood and the decision that then may need implementing can be further assessed at a case conference or school review meeting. The supervisor must know what the line of decision making and accountability is, but more important, must be sure that the worker is comfortable with the assessment and preliminary decisions that have been made in supervision. It is the worker who is likely to have to share with the case conference the basis on which the assessment has been made, as well as to implement any decision.

The Implications of Inadequate Supervision

Failure to offer a 'safe space' within which appropriate supervision can be carried on will result in the worker carrying the full weight of responsibility for any families' incompetence or violence, as well as the rage and helplessness of associated interested parties. The end result will be anger, frustration and guilt; effective work will suffer and the eventual negative spin-off will be felt by the worker, the profession and of course the family. Nor do I find the term 'supportive supervision' adequate to the process which I shall describe. Support alone may be collusive or unenlightened and will leave the problem with the worker who is in the firing line. If supervision fails to free the worker it can be said to be inadequate. We have all had experience of supervisors who remove the work or decision making from us, and as supervisors we know how tempting it is to do just that. Michael Mercer, writing in a paper on 'professional development in social work' speaks of the need for social workers to take responsibility for their own motivation for being in the profession. This involves being prepared to face those parts of themselves which are often hidden but which our clients present to us as their problem. Mercer writes: [4]

> Offering clients insight which is not firmly rooted in self awareness is ultimately persecutory even if the insight is accurate because the client is not helped to bear the pain of their new knowledge. . . . we suffer as clients do and we share their humanity.

Some of the Processes Operating in Casework

I now want to move on to naming some of the processes which are operating in all relationship work and which, if not understood, can result in workers being baffled and overwhelmed. Clearly naming a process is not enough, for we are talking about creative work going forward with our most difficult clients. If we can disentangle and understand some of these processes in supervision we can begin to identify the focus for work within a particular family.

Transference

Transference is the process whereby we invest important people in our immediate lives with the feelings we had towards significant others (usually our parents) in our past. The more damaged or insecure we are the more painful these feelings can be, especially when they are not understood. The need to transfer those feelings (from the person we once knew) to others is a mechanism which helps us to deal with the full impact of those early childhood emotions. We project these early feelings into the present as a way of avoiding the full implication of those feelings. Understanding this mechanism becomes crucial when the experiences of early childhood have been especially painful and so we transfer our feelings about a poor mothering experience to an adult woman in the present who is in a mothering/caring relationship with us. For example: it is too awful for a woman to recognise that her mother rejected her at birth and failed to care for her so she 'turns' her female social worker into 'mother' whom she can then punish by ensuring that she is 'no good'.

The process of transference is common to us all. It is, I believe, an unconscious event in all human relationships and is not restricted to some esoteric therapeutic experience, for we meet each other with both the conscious and the unconscious aspects of ourselves. For all of us, our past is part of our present. [5]

If we fail to recognise transference as a phenomenon we are in trouble, for we are failing to understand a most primitive dynamic in ourselves and others. Transference is closely linked to what we know about separation from the writings of Bowlby, Robertson and others. Jane Temperley writes: [6]

> We are all taught that people feel anger and a sense of desertion when left by someone they value and that people who have been repeatedly let down and disappointed experience even their worker going on holiday for a couple of weeks as a desertion which may make it impossible for them to continue to trust and work with that worker. Yet all of us at times I think find ourselves amazed at re-discovering just how powerfully our clients feel about our absences. They continually teach us the reality of what is in danger of becoming just theoretical knowledge to us.

This theoretical knowledge has to become reality in our practice both as individuals as well as a team, or we will be overwhelmed and professionally disenchanted by the rejections by our clients and criticisms of our colleagues.

Projective Identification

The phenomenon of transference is also inextricably linked to that of projective identification, for the feelings which really belong to the client are being actually experienced by the worker. These feelings can stem from early relationships but they are manifested as emotionally powerful in the present. In the example of negative transference given above, the worker begins to feel she is the bad, uncaring mother that her client once had and she will begin to believe she is a bad, uncaring worker unless she can be helped to see that the emotions do not in fact belong to her. Similarly and even more subtly a client can tell a worker how marvellous he or she is and how awful the last worker was. How easily we all fall into the trap of patting ourselves on the back and criticising our predecessor or the referring agency! In fact the client who is congratulating in this unreal way is usually saying more about how bad she feels about deserting, uncaring parents and how anxious she is to be the good child so you, the new worker, do not leave her too.

Jane Temperley in a paper given to the first British-American Conference on Psychodynamic Social Work says: [7]

> Projective identification is an unconscious mechanism whereby experiences which are felt to be unmanageable are disowned, largely by

eliciting those experiences and emotions in others. It is a mechanism we all resort to in varying degrees and the more disturbed we are, the more we will be using it. The mother, who as a girl and as a wife always had to be compliant, may unconsciously elicit in her own daughter the demanding angry attitudes she herself repudiated and which she can now condemn in the daughter as she did and does in herself.

When I move on to more extensive case material later in this paper I hope I can demonstrate that these processes not only go on within families but also between the individual client (or whole family) and the worker. The aim of creative supervision is to tease out these processes and discuss how the mechanism can best be understood and appropriately worked with. Sometimes, for the worker to understand the process is enough. As he comes to understand, he will be less of a victim. In other situations he may actually try and interpret to the client something of what he feels the client is unconsciously saying. For example, in the situation where a mother makes the worker feel that she is the client's own bad mother, it may be appropriate simply to understand the process. However, it may be more therapeutic to comment: 'It seems I can never do anything right, I wonder if you are trying to punish me'.

But supervision is more than identifying processes, for the task is not simply to produce an accurate account of the dynamics of the family but rather to enable the worker to separate out what belongs to the family from what belongs to the worker's own life experiences and inner world. Creative work can only go forward as the processes are understood and a focus for work can be decided upon.

Countertransference

Countertransference may be the key to determining the focus of work and enabling such work to go forward. Countertransference is the term used to describe those feelings aroused in the worker by the client. Traditional social work teaching of a decade and more ago warned us of our own personal neuroses getting into the work and we were advised to have no feelings and to remain detached! Many of us rejected that view because we recognised that we often could not avoid feelings for our seductive and damaged clients. Maybe we swung too far from clinical aloofness and became over-involved and as enmeshed in the problems and personalities as our families were themselves. Either way the feelings which we undoubtedly had when confronted with difficult family situations, often involving children who were being abused or neglected, were not considered as an aid to work.

Once again I will quote Jane Temperley: [7]

> Of course workers of all levels of sophistication must be constantly
> vigilant in examining how our own personal neuroses are affecting our
> response to clients . . . We no longer think that these emotions are just
> an interference to be cleared up in the worker's personal self-
> examination. We are much more inclined to view the counter-
> transference as an invaluable source of information about what the client
> is unconsciously projecting into the worker and thereby signalling is of
> crucial importance in his predicament. Countertranference in Freud's
> original sense, indicated what is personal to the worker, whereas we
> have come to use the term primarily as meaning what is elicited in the
> worker by the client, in an attempt to rid himself of it and also
> unconsciously to communicate to the worker what the core pain is. It
> seems to me that projective identification can be seen as one of the most
> powerful and primitive means of communication that human beings
> have and if understood, potentially a very valuable one.

If countertransference is to become that powerful tool of communication the worker must feel safe enough within the supervisory
relationship to give expression to those feelings. If a worker
confesses to feeling no good, to having done something stupid or
collusive with the client, it is all too easy to forget and excuse. These
adjectives are the language of guilt whereas the misdeeds (if such
indeed they are) are more creatively used as information and
indications of how the family experiences its own pain and problems.
A worker who can admit to feeling helpless and overwhelmed by the
problems of any family is far more in touch with that family's needs,
than the worker who can spell out all the umpteen lines of communication with other agencies, but cannot determine the specific areas of
work that need to be undertaken.

The words just quoted 'of course workers of all levels of sophisti-
cation must be constantly vigilant in examining how our own personal
neuroses are affecting our response to clients . . .' [7] must never be
overlooked. The pendulum would have again swung too far if we
identified all feelings as belonging only to the client under discussion.
For example, a worker spoke of her client's rather unreal depression
over the loss of a child more than ten years ago. The worker seemed
depressed but somewhat bewildered by her identification with her
client, whose problems seemed to be much more contemporary and
concerned with the management of rather delinquent adolescent
sons. In supervision we realised that the client was hooking into the
quite considerable latent depression of the worker. The worker's loss

of her marriage and the feeling that she had lost her child-bearing potential had come to the surface and was in some small way interfering with her ability to decide on the focus for work. In the event it was decided that the focus should be the mother's feelings about losing control of her sons as they grew up and how their delinquent behaviour might be understood as arising from their need for separation from this controlling mother.

So if countertransference is to become the central tool for understanding client feeling then the personal feelings, blind-spots and pains of workers must first be acknowledged.

The Triangle of the Psychodynamics Process

So the triangle is completed, transference originating from one person's past life being projected on to the 'other', and now that 'other' (the social worker) feeling and knowing in himself the pain of these confused, interrelated and unconscious processes. If the client's inner world and unconscious transactions are a triangle, a triangle also exists between the worker, the supervisor and the client. This secondary triangle is described by Janet Mattinson in *The Reflection Process in Casework Supervision.* [8] She describes in detail through the use of social workers' training groups how 'the worker–client relationship and the worker–supervisor relationship will sometimes mirror each other and that work clarifying feelings in one relationship has the effect of making clear what is happening in the other.'

Casework Examples

I now want to take some material from my own supervision. I want to try and demonstrate how the above theory can be used to understand unconscious processes in family work, in order that particular families may experience improved well-being.

Daisy
First an example of negative transference with massive projective identification. Daisy was a West Indian middle-aged woman with three children. We knew little if anything of her background or the father of the children. Annabelle the eldest child was now pregnant and the mental health social worker who had known the family for ten years was being promoted and leaving the area. On his own admission he had achieved little but we all recognised that he was the only significant male adult Daisy knew.

For weeks if not months after the transfer to FSU Daisy played angry, complex games with the new worker. She criticised, blamed and complained. Everything the old worker had done was miraculous; everything the new worker did was useless. She asked for rehousing, Christmas food parcels, decoration of her flat, and letters to the Department of Health and Social Security, each time asserting 'that's what Mr. W. did'. The worker tried to stay with her relationship with Daisy; asking Daisy to take a part in each letter or telephone call. Each time she opted out, screaming that she was not being helped because she was black or mad. The worker managed to go on visiting, pointing out occasionally how difficult she was to help. The initiative to visit was always with the FSU worker whereas previously it had been with Daisy who had had to go and demand action on her own behalf. The FSU worker was not driven away by Daisy's angry demands and continuous criticism. She was able to separate out, with Daisy, problems that belonged to Daisy herself and problems which rightly belonged to Annabelle, the daughter. In addition, the worker was able to mourn the lost and now idealised previous social worker.

When Annabelle's child was born there was concern for the baby whilst mother and grandmother fought over its care. Over a year later Daisy could discuss her need to mother the new grandchild, and let Annabelle be mother whilst she remained its grandmother/ foster-mother, and the whole family could laugh with the worker about how difficult Daisy can be. Our understanding of the negative transference in this case helped the worker to stay in the family when all the screaming might have meant that an unsupported worker would have reverted to the previous model of intervention — 'Come and see us if ever you have a problem'. As well as having a much easier home to be in, the family became far more able to determine its own life-style, cope with major and minor irritations and use social work help positively. The social worker, by dealing with Daisy's rage about the lost idealised worker was able to reach some of her very lost, rejected feelings of childhood and by quite simple acknowledgment made them less destructive in the present.

It is relatively simple to write that cameo of Daisy and her growing family but infinitely more difficult to describe the process in supervision that effected the change in Daisy and her family (see Janet Mattinson's *The Deadly Equal Triangle* [9]). The worker came to the case immediately after completing a qualifying course. She was eager to demonstrate that in spite of her relative inexperience she would not be overwhelmed by 'heavy' cases. However, Daisy got to the very heart of this anxiety. Her constant shouting, belittling and idealisation of the previous worker were just the areas the new worker did not want to handle. The worker needed the safe space of supervision to own her anxieties about her own value. With regard to Daisy's constant rejections of the worker, I kept saying 'Stay with it — don't leave, for that will confirm her worst fears that she is too mad for anyone to tolerate'. This advice stemmed from my knowledge of projective identification, for if the worker left the case she would have acted out the deep fear in the client that 'mother abandons you if you are too demanding'. However, what I did not know until supervision was that the worker had fears of her own stemming from the loss of her own mother when she was very young. The worker was anxious as to how she was being perceived in her team — was she as mad and disturbed as Daisy? To deny this worker the experience of her own root pain, which was triggered off by having regular contact with Daisy, would have resulted in the end in the worker leaving family work. In the event she could 'stay with it'; she could recognise that she could face and manage her own deprivation experiences and as a result was able to go on working with Daisy.

A further aspect of the supervision of Daisy was a deepening understanding of my relationship with the worker and the feelings I had as the work was presented. The worker pointed out her anxiety about this family, often making me feel as bemused as she was. I had known the previous worker and felt angry that he had just left this family to us, apparently having achieved so little. It was weeks before I could see that my anger with him for dumping the family on us was effectively preventing me from helping the worker to cope with Daisy's feelings of being dumped and abandoned.

The progress in this case, as I have already intimated, is that Daisy is beginning to be able to receive and even give. She has accepted some furniture which became available. Somehow before, nothing was right. Most satisfying of all she had been to a Unit party and had a good time, leading others in a knees up! She had been able to let go her depression and despair, and the effect is that her three children are less neglected and deprived. 'It is more blessed to give than to receive' (Acts 20, v.35) but we cannot give from an empty cupboard, and Daisy along with so many of our families had never received anything for herself. She had no resources from which to give. There is enormous satisfaction for the social worker if he can be part of the process which liberates and enables clients to learn to give. They are then more in control of themselves and their environment and not simply the victims of their own unconscious needs or the rage of a helpless community.

Perhaps this description of the work with Daisy seems too trite. She is more of an individual than a family and the work has largely been focused on Daisy herself. Before moving on to a more complex family situation, I want to say a brief word about idealisation.

I have already mentioned how Daisy idealised her previous worker and how eventually the new worker was able to help Daisy mourn his going. Idealisation of lost objects is part of the transference and projective identification mechanism described earlier. Originally a Kleinian concept, the client idealises a lost parent or parent figure. The process of idealisation is a defence against feeling the actual pain associated with the loss of that person. A client will speak of the dead parent as 'ideal and marvellous' and in this way will hide from the rage and pain of being abandoned by that mother on her death. If it is the previous worker who is idealised, there is similar fear of acknow-ledging that there was real pain in his leaving – and perhaps the fearful hidden fantasy that the worker left because the client was so bad or destructive. In the situation with Daisy, the worker had con-tinually to acknowledge how much Daisy genuinely missed her previous worker, as well as saying that perhaps she was fearful he had gone just because she was so demanding. Simultaneously Daisy could not really believe that a worker would make a regular weekly commitment to visit, and would return, especially when she herself had been so consistently angry and rejecting. It took months of acknowledging these fears (and speculation in supervision about this powerful process) before we learnt how she had been abandoned by her husband and had been sent from the West Indies to this country as a child because she was too difficult at home. Daisy's fear of her own destructiveness, her fear of what she might do to her children and her grandchildren had successfully crippled her for years.

The Carey Family

The Carey family has baffled and overwhelmed social workers and the local caring agencies in the community for years. (Even as I write this I am advised by my team that the family is too complex and the work so unsuccessful that they should not be presented.) But I believe they are not untypical of families worked with both by FSU and by many workers in social services departments.

Mr and Mrs Carey have four young children. They live in a too small, ground-floor flat. Mr Carey is one of seventeen siblings, although there is no known contact with his family of origin. He has an unskilled job for which he is very poorly paid. He has, we under-stand, been previously married but we know nothing of his previous family. Mrs Carey also comes from a large family of eight children, and we know little more of her past. The Careys present as a 'multi-problem family'. I say this advisedly, because one has to question whether the problems are experienced as more acute by the supporting agencies than by the family itself. However, whilst we concern ourselves with childcare issues, prevention of eviction, and school attendance problems, the family are struggling with day-to-day management of practical and financial matters. Mrs Carey appears completely overwhelmed by the problems of cooking, washing and caring for the house and family. The end results which present to us as 'the problems' are that the rent and electricity never get paid, the children never go to school — or go anywhere which means getting up, getting dressed or being on time. For years a social worker has been in the family; play therapy has been given to each child in turn to try and offer them individual space to build up their ego strength; a series of community service volunteers have known the family, taking the younger children to day nurseries and some-times helping with household chores in an attempt to give Mrs Carey some structure to her life. Both Mrs Carey and the eldest child have been in groups at the Unit at various times but the problem was always that they 'didn't come', couldn't be ready and their lateness enraged other members of the groups for being kept waiting or losing group time. The hand-to-mouth existence of this family with the threat of eviction (for nonpayment of rent), fuel supply disconnec-tion (for non-payment of bills) and reception into care (for non-school attendance) has been a constant anxiety to the social worker. Mrs Carey will barrage workers with words, usually blaming the bad weather for her inability to get up, get children dressed, get to rent office, etc. etc. Mr Carey will blame his wife for her incompetence and encourage the children to do the same. His income is low; he gives even less to his wife to manage on, opts out of all responsibility in the home and is frequently drunk.

The reader might well ask 'where do you start?' Initially it is important to identify how hopeless the worker feels (and indeed the whole Unit team) and realise that the family feels similarly over-whelmed by the hopelessness. We can as easily resort to blaming Mr Carey for being a bad husband and father as Mrs Carey blames the weather or the school for being too far away. The key to effective work must be to look at individual incidents and sessions and see what can be learnt. It is important to tease out the psychodynamic pro-cesses that are operating; to test out our suppositions about how the family feels by how the worker feels (and the supervisor too) and to be sure that no personal blind-spots are leading the worker (or supervisor) to concentrate on red herrings, or to seek magic answers in alternative techniques. It is all too easy to be seduced into 'a flight from intractable despair into technical skill, used as a defence'. [4] One incident we discussed in supervision concerned the electricity bill. Mrs Carey had handed it to the worker, saying 'Here's the electricity bill, my last social worker didn't pay it'. The worker felt baffled. She was quite sure the previous worker had not just paid a bill on demand but now she was being expected to do so. She also felt angry. The family had refused to discuss any serious problems over the past two months, nor would they do anything constructive to improve their poor financial situation. Mr Carey was obviously doing something illegal which prevented him having wage slips, so the worker could not get rent or rate rebates, family income supplement, or any other benefit designed for low-income families. What benefits they did receive were given by the good offices of concerned professionals who waived aside the formalities of means testing. She also felt anxious. She was an experienced worker but relatively new to both the agency and the family, and perhaps after all she was not as competent as her predecessor? We developed this one small incident as far as we could, to try and understand better how the family ticked, and then to focus more acutely on the right areas for work.

Using the feelings we were experiencing as this discussion continued, I realised that the worker was dumping the problem of the electricity bill on to me in much the same way as the client had done to her the week before. She was now feeling baffled and angered by the family and also anxious that I, her relatively new supervisor, might criticise her for not being able to handle such an apparently simple situation. Together we got in touch with our anxiety that maybe the previous worker was better. We began to see that I was idealising the past worker in much the same way as Mrs Carey was doing. I was angry that she had left and angry too that she had not been a better worker. (My fantasy is always that if I were a better supervisor the workers would be perfect and would never leave!!) Mrs Carey also felt that if she had been 'better' the previous worker would never have left (nor all her predecessors). She could not bear to acknowledge these feelings of anger at having been deserted so she produced a bill which 'the last worker did not pay'. This idealisation of the past worker with the accompanying unacknowledged rage led us to speculate about Mrs Carey's childhood and her longing to have both the perfect mother she never had, and the opportunity to express the feelings of rage she has never been able to own about being so badly let down as a child. In the event, the worker used the opportunity to begin to mourn the last worker. As Mrs Carey could express her anger about being left so she could begin to give expression to 'no-one ever does anything to help'. It was the other side of the same coin — a longing that the perfect parent would miraculously make everything better — but we were now able to look at how all the family undermined all the 'help' they were offered.

Mr Carey is so easily left out of the discussion (both here and in supervision) and this itself serves as an indication of what it must be like to have seventeen siblings. We could hardly bring ourselves to look at his part in the undermining of the help being offered to the family. For the first time we got in touch with his rage at never getting enough, and began to understand why he needed to belittle women (his wife and the family worker). The worker needed supervision not only to examine this process but to discover how she could work with Mr Carey without becoming persecutory and blaming. She herself had feelings from her own family situation about men who had no imagination and were trapped in the status quo. Now she was being asked to work with a man who was so frightened of growing up that he escaped into drink if ever asked 'to take his responsibilities seriously'. For Mr Carey to 'grow up' would mean more responsibilities; it would mean using his wife as a partner and equal rather than punishing her for not meeting his expectations of the ideal mother. From one small incident the worker has been able to find various foci for work and is no longer so totally overwhelmed as she was previously.

There is no success story to end this account of work with the Carey family. School attendance remains poor and there have been incidents of bruising to one child. Our level of anxiety and stress is lower because we are beginning to understand some of the forces at work in the family and so work can be focused a bit more accurately. This is allowing new methods of work to be introduced which are designed to value and involve Mr Carey. We have not escaped into alternative techniques out of desperation.

'Burnt-Out' Workers

Social workers all too often leave the field or accept promotion because they are burnt out. They feel they have reached the limit of their own resources. They are frustrated, irritated and disenchanted. The Carey family has been responsible for many able staff saying 'But what about the Careys?'. Workers can feel helpless and overwhelmed by the intractability of the problems and occasionally we are tempted to forget the many strengths the family has. As we have difficulty remembering the strengths the family has, we have equal difficulty hanging on to our own strengths and skills. Perhaps one of the crucial aspects of supervision is the self-esteem of the worker (and the supervisor). The worker needs to be truly valued, not just given platitudinous reassurances. Doubts in the work have to be tested out again and again with a properly thought-through theoretical framework and often the worker will need to know that a particular crises is not so out of the ordinary.

Decision Making, Crises and Controls

Another constantly recurring theme in supervision is that concerned with control, decision making and power. The problem is how to get the potency back into the family when statutory forces are at work removing the decision-making powers from a family. So often this powerlessness is hard to recognise for its origins can be very innocent. A decision is made to place in a nursery a child thought perhaps to be at risk of physical injury. The parent is not likely to know that such nursery places are at a premium and she will just be relieved that she has a 'good' social worker or health visitor who got the child so placed.

In one family we know, the child was placed, the parents were both in work and no payments were made. In spite of repeated recommendations from FSU to the contrary, the place was kept open with outstanding payments owing amounting to hundreds of pounds. Only months later did it transpire that the family faced eviction because for the third time they have accrued £400 in rent arrears. For too long the family have been protected from the reality of the world in which they live. It now falls to the social worker to 'do' something for this family, who are on the verge of eviction with signs that the marriage is disintegrating. But what to do and how to advise in such a situation? The family have been constantly protected from reality and the task for the social worker must be to allow them and herself to experience the pain of the real world. In this case there is marital breakdown, and children who are constantly left at home alone while their mother is out. The worker finds it almost impossible to meet the mother, has never met the father and if she allows herself to feel too close to the situation she will find herself carrying the whole weight of the children's sense of desolation. I believe there are no short cuts. The pain has to be experienced and shared. If a short cut is taken — and the children are removed on the grounds that they are often unattended — then the cycle of protection from reality will be repeated. In such a situation the worker must stay as close as possible at the time of eviction, whilst asking how such a situation might be avoided in future.

There are other decisions that are made which can have equally far reaching implications. Decisions to recommend a child for special school or boarding school; decisions to refer a child for play therapy or psychiatric help; and the most difficult of all to handle, the decision to exclude a child from school. In many of these situations the decision has been made at case conferences, review meetings or occasionally by individuals. The social worker may or may not have been involved. However, it is usually the social worker who is asked to implement the decision and 'do something' after the decision has been made. Time and again he is also left to work with the parents who may well not have been party to the decision. In a recent supervision session my conversation with a very experienced social worker went a bit like this:

Worker:	'Johnny has been recommended for boarding school; all his behaviour suggests that he wants to be away from his family and the education authorities feel that only a boarding school would enable him to make any educational progress. My problem now is to help the family see that this is what they want themselves for Johnny.'
Supervisor:	'But it is not what they want for Johnny. They are very angry about Johnny's behaviour and feel it puts them in a bad light. They can't bear to feel they are incompetent parents.'
Worker:	'True, but it is important that they are involved in the decision or Johnny will never get to school.'
Supervisor:	'True. I think Johnny and his parents both need stronger boundaries and limits. You are able to see that it is in Johnny's best interest that he go to a special school. He needs the extra care, security, consistency that the school will give him. Your anxiety about getting something extra for Johnny contributed to the final recommendation that he should go away. Now the dilemma is to help the parents look at Johnny's needs for themselves. Don't feed their bad image of themselves but rather expect them to want the very best for each of their children.'

Following a session like this the worker was able to be much clearer about the decision to send Johnny away to school and more importantly to be experienced as effective by the family. If the worker simply 'implements decisions' he will be seen by the clients to be only a yes-man, making happen decisions in which neither he nor they had a part. If full discussions do not accompany such decisions the outcome will become even more complex with truancy, delinquency or school refusal complicating the family dynamics.

The reverse situation can also occur when the client takes overall control and then plays angry games for fear of losing control.

Mr Larch had a history of manic depressive illness and Mrs Larch could become acutely depressed and drink to excess. The teenage son of the marriage had a few 'outbursts', running away from home or overdosing. This tight, almost incestuous family was totally inter-dependent and each blamed another member for the difficulties. Mr Larch tried to control his family and the louder he shouted the more they rejected him. The worker felt she too was going out of control, becoming manic and ineffective. In supervision she could identify her own controls and strengths again and so work with Mr Larch on his controls. Her line, quite appropriately was, 'until you get yourself under control (by appropriate medication in this case) you can't blame the rest of the family if they ignore your attempts to control them'. The son had always rejected any social work involvement for himself, saying he wasn't mad like his parents. When the decision was made to engage him in an individual therapeutic relationship (following an overdose incident) he first banged angrily out of the room and later arranged a whole series of appointments with his new worker which he then failed to attend. Our understanding of this process is that Dick (the boy) has deep anxieties about loss of control going back to early childhood experiences of deprivation and separation. It is unlikely that these roots of pain and anxiety will ever be explored but the worker must speculate about them to enable him not to get caught in the same trap himself. He needs to engage Dick without shouting or persecuting; by acknowledging his fear of being let down or even abandoned and in time perhaps his fear of madness (ultimate loss of control).

Having written the above account of the Larch family I read it to Joe, the worker allocated to engage Dick in a therapeutic relationship. So many games were being played that both the family worker and Joe felt under strain, with everyone else (GP, child psychiatrist, medical social worker and hospital chaplain) feeling excluded from the family and helpless. Joe said the importance of supervision for him was that he could get in touch with his own fears about loss of control which would go some way to explaining Dick's need to over-control. For Joe the anxiety about loss of control was not about madness (as we suppose it is for Dick) but rather about loss of order and a predictable outcome. Because of his own difficulties in establishing work with Dick he could understand the feelings of other caring professionals who wanted to help and then were angry at their impotence.

Another very common area of crisis concerns the request to receive a child into care. A recent case concerned a father who refused to look after his child whilst his wife was in hospital having their second baby. In his request Mr Hall was saying something very forceful about his anxiety about having children. He was able to own the deep rivalry he felt with his two year-old (for affection) and his demand for reception into care for his child also enabled him to speak of his own experience of being rejected and put in care when very young. Meanwhile the social worker in this family was bemused and anxious because it was his first case in a new agency which 'blew up' within a few days of contact. He felt it was his fault. The supervisor has to be relaxed enough not to add to that self-blaming, but rather think through the process and needs of that family and help identify the areas needing to be worked with at the time. The worker told me that the supervision on this incident was helpful in a number of respects. First he was reassured that this type of crisis often occurs early in a contact and that it was in no way his fault. This enabled us to examine what the client was saying by his action and demands. This reassurance was also experienced as 'giving permission for the problem to exist'. Part of the worker's self-reproach stemmed from the fear that urgent requests for reception into care simply did not happen in FSU — after all, wasn't one of the aims of a preventative agency to avoid reception into care? The worker also told me it was important to him that I had been able to imagine myself into how he was feeling. His initial reaction had been anger with Mr Hall for not being able to look after his two year-old son, feeling that he himself would have made a better father. Later he was able to recognise how difficult it was for Mr Hall to father his child. His whole life experience mitigated against him ever being able to love and care for a dependent child. Once the worker was given permission to have difficulties he could then go back to the father and find the actual care of the child quite anxiety-making. The two men struggled with nappies and wondered together if the child would ever stop crying. It was then that the breakthrough in the work came; the relationship between the worker and the Hall family was thoroughly cemented; the child spent a brief period in care and when the second child was eventually born a further reception into care was not needed or asked for.

Supervision within a Team Setting and the Varying Styles of Workers and Supervisors

I spelt out at the beginning my basic definition of supervision as a safe space where the worker and supervisor together can focus on the needs of the family, using their own personalities to increase the effectiveness of this task. It should also be said that each worker's style will vary as will the style of each supervisor. It is important that supervisors recognise and identify their own style and occasionally check with their social workers that they feel comfortable enough to work well in supervision. My own style is fairly directive. Sometimes the only way I can think myself well enough into a situation is to speculate how a worker might respond to a client, giving them an actual sentence or framework of a conversation. My team tell me that this both enables them to hang on to the main areas of work they want to keep in mind, and frees them to experiment with different approaches to a client. For instance in the Carey family, the worker told me how exasperated she was with everyone blaming the other for not waking each other up each morning so that the children could get to school. Mr Carey always got up but somehow never succeeded in waking his wife so that she could get the children up. The worker felt she was slipping into the same persecutory merry-go-round. I suggested that she tell Elizabeth (the eldest child) that blaming her mother was not the point. That it was *her* responsibility to get up in the morning and there was no point in blaming her mother for not waking her. She, Elizabeth herself, would have to take the consequences of perpetual absences from school. In the event the worker broke the cycle, started taking Elizabeth to school herself, so that a new pattern could be established and Elizabeth could discuss her feelings about the difficulties of getting up to go to school. In no way did I *tell* the worker this was a modelling task she had to perform. Rather, in putting the responsibility back on the child, each member of the family could begin to take some small responsibility for their own behaviour.

Supervision of individual workers cannot be done in isolation from the team, particularly when a worker may be sharing material which is deeply personal to himself. It needs to be said that I in no way regard supervision as psychotherapy for staff. Any relationship which is open, honest and shared will have a therapeutic quality to it. Should a worker want to explore in depth problems in his own inner world, or experience disabling relationships with his own family or peers, then I would suggest he sees a psychotherapist for his own needs. Having said this, one cannot avoid the issue of confidentiality. With clients who manipulate and tell a duty worker something 'in secret' our standard reply is 'we don't have secrets from one another'. However, in supervision my stance is somewhat different, and if a confidence is shared, I would then ask who else in the team knows or how can it best be shared. When discussing this section with a member of my team she replied, 'I can share something personal in supervision and the fact that it is a safe space where I will not be criticised gives me permission to go and share it with others'. The Unit actually structures into the week a team meeting where feelings and emotions — positive and negative — can be shared in the whole group when and as the members of that group feel secure enough so to share. The group meeting will range in discussion from a member telling how she experienced the team's support when her grand-mother died to others asking if someone felt supported enough over a particularly anxious incident in a case.

Regular assessment of how a worker is performing is also a matter for both individual supervision and team discussion. I would hope that staff will always want evaluation and feedback, both in their role as individual workers and as to how they are experienced within the team. This assessment will only be effective if the 'confidential' or 'personal' issues have been appropriately handled prior to the actual assessment. Sometimes it is important for the supervisor to feed back to the group particular areas of difficulty a worker may be having, but more often assessment serves as a time of evaluating work done and discussing expectations for the future.

More about Working as a Whole Team
At Queens Park FSU we have the joys and problems of what we term 'cross working'. Workers will see their clients by regular appointment in the traditional way. But often clients want more than the once a week contact and so will come to the Unit 'to see the social worker'. We try and have a duty social worker available to answer the door and deal with pressing phone calls. On a practical level we try to be as well informed as possible about the needs of each other's clients, but on an emotional level there are many confused and treacherous waters to pass. Clients can idealise and fantasise about their own worker (when he is not there) leaving the duty worker

feeling impotent and useless. Subtle games of manipulation can be played. . . . 'my worker said I could. . .' and the confusion that results in the staff team can be enormous. One worker can be blamed or feel blamed that all his clients are causing the duty worker to do a lot of running around. The duty worker might feel criticised by the social worker for not managing the situation in just the way the actual worker would have done. The convolutions of these situations are enormous, and they need to be unravelled between individuals in the team as well as in the whole staff group. To fail to do this will result in staff feeling angry and burnt out. Sometimes this unravelling process will start within the safety of individual supervision but then move on to the weekly team meeting when feelings are discussed.

Team Leadership and Caseload Management

In a small team where the team leader does all the staff supervision there is less likelihood of confused lines of decision making and mismanagement. However, as a social worker is rarely better than his or her supervisor, neither can a team be better than its leader. For creative work to go on with families in distress there needs to be an overview of caseloads as well as a clear view of individual cases.

The first aspect of this caseload management concerns time. If whole families are to be seen regularly, how can evening work best be planned and what arrangements are made in regard to time taken in lieu of overtime worked? If proper arrangements are not made then workers will surely 'burn out' and leave the agency angrily after all too short a time. Whilst considering the demands of evening work I would also consider the whole subject of 'how long does any piece of work take' and are the expectations put on the worker realistic? I would also expect a team consensus for what is realistic. Our view is that no worker should work more than three evenings per week and of those evenings only one should be after 8.00 pm. We build in one morning off a week for all staff and other time off is taken when possible.

As well as these issues of time there are also those concerning realistic workloads. In FSU we try and offer workers as wide a range of work as possible, within the limitations of the nature of referrals. So if a severely depressed single mother is referred we would hope to allocate her to someone with enough space to take on another depressed client. The same applies to very disorganised families, acting-out adolescents and families with known drinking problems. There is always likely to be some overlap, but an overview needs to be kept so that caseloads do not become lopsided and work repetitive and unstimulating. Also there needs to be an integral view of all work, not simply a caseload. Groups, play therapy, family therapy, duty and student supervision all take time, energy and expertise. All work needs recording and evaluating and most areas of work will be supervised independently from casework supervision.

Conclusion

The title of this paper concerns the prevention of 'burn out' in social workers working under pressure. All too often social workers feel as abused, overwhelmed and battered as the families they are trying to help. If this process is not understood and grappled with in detail we can only say that as a profession we are inadequately equipped for the task we have set ourselves to achieve. I can only hope that I have demonstrated sufficiently clearly and completely, that until we examine the processes which are operating in any given situation, and learn how the worker's feelings and personality fit into those of the family under stress, we should not be too surprised when workers leave the scene disenchanted and exhausted. I can do no better than to end with a further quotation from Jane Temperley: [7]

> I think it cannot be too much stressed that the unconscious does not cease to operate simply because we decide we are not equipped to interpret it . . . . It may perhaps not be appropriate . . . for the workers . . . to make interpretations to their clients about what they are projecting into them. It does seem to me, however, crucial that they have access via consultation or supervision to a perspective that frees them to comprehend rather than to be taken over by their clients' repudiated experience.

References

1. J. Mattinson, *The Deadly Equal Triangle*. Paper given at the first British/American Conference on Psychodynamic Social Work. GAPS, 1979.

2. S. Hornby, *The Place of Psychotherapy in Social Work*. GAPS, 1973.

3. G. Blech, 'Supervision'. *FSU Quarterly*. Winter 1977, pp. 1–6.

4. M. Mercer, *Professional Development in Social Work*. GAPS, 1981.

5. J. F. Knight, *Transference and Counter Transference in Social Work*. GAPS, 1978.

6. J. Temperley, *The Implications for the Teaching of Psychodynamics on Basic Social Work Courses.* GAPS, 1977.

7. J. Temperley, *The Implications for Social Work Practice of Recent Psychoanalytic Development.* Paper given at the first British/American Conference on Psychodynamic Social Work. GAPS, 1979.

8. J. Mattinson, *The Reflection Process in Casework Supervision,* p. 7. Institute of Marital Studies/Tavistock, 1975.

9. J. Mattinson, *The Deadly Equal Triangle.* Paper given at the first British/American Conference on Psychodynamic Social Work. GAPS, 1979.

GAPS. Group for the Advancement of Psychodynamics and Psychotherapy in Social Work. Papers can be obtained from the Secretary, 3, Romilly Road, London N4.

2. A Unitary Approach to Teamwork: Some Payoffs and Pitfalls

David Horn and Rosemary Clews

The aim of this paper is to describe the process of movement towards a unitary approach within the East Birmingham Unit. This movement had caused us to challenge our ways of thinking about people with problems, ways of organising, supervising and working together as a team. We hope that an account of some of the pitfalls encountered will be helpful to others who may be following a similar path.

Outline of Structure
As our title indicates, we do not accept that there is one definitive unitary approach, so we initially state our understanding and definition. We continue with an outline of our starting point in the Unit, and move to a consideration of what the approach has meant for our team practice within the agency. We then look at what the pressures for change were, how we established some priorities, a review of some pitfalls encountered, and how we overcame some obstacles and began to hold together a number of developmental strands. The second main section reviews some implications for inter-agency issues, particularly how we wrestled with the need for workers to be community-oriented without losing their commitment to the agency. Thirdly, we give an overview of the changes. In our concluding section we outline particular strategies we have used.

Unitary Approach – Aims and Definitions
This section gives the theoretical base of our work, and shows how we looked at the unitary approach in practice. We give our definitions, and seek to relate them to values and to the kinds of work we believe to be important. Of necessity, we have used condensed definitions, but for a fuller description we refer the reader to Pincus and Minahan. [1] Four major concepts are used by these writers to

explain the unitary approach: client system, action system, change agent and target system.

The term 'client system' refers to those who are expected to benefit from the social work service. Agreement between those potential beneficiaries and the worker is essential. This is, of course, a departure from the usual definition of 'client', as this term usually refers to all recipients of social work service, whether or not an agreement has been made between them and the social worker. In our Unit we try to maintain the distinction between 'clients' and those with whom we have not reached an agreement. If an individual group or family is referred to us, and we consider the referral appropriate, they become 'potential clients' and we open the work for enquiry. If an agreement can be made with the potential client, work is formally opened, and our potential client becomes an actual client.

The 'action system' comprises the social worker and the people he or she works with, or through, to accomplish the tasks, and achieve the agreed goals. [2] Our action systems include both professionals and non-professionals, volunteers and paid staff. In our experience other family members, local clergy and relatives are at least as significant in the work as the professionals. Case conferences are usually planning meetings, where both the client system and much of the action system are present: a meeting where agreements are made, clarified or changed between the helpers and the client system, and between the different members of the action system. We find that it gives dignity to a person with an agency 'client' label to be a co-worker on agreed tasks, and not merely a passive recipient of service. For many clients this has been a crucial way of enabling them to accept confrontation on sensitive issues.

We use Leonard's definition [3] of the 'change agent' as the person or group *responsible* for deliberately pursuing the stated goal of the social work service. The social worker nominated as 'key worker' within the Unit is invariably the change agent, and often takes on the role of co-ordinating the efforts of all those who make up the action system.

Finally, the 'target system' is the system that must change if the agreed goals are to be achieved. Traditionally, the target for change is the person or family referred to a social work agency. The unitary model as we interpret it encourages us to look for the most appropriate target for change. A child who is not succeeding in school, for example, may be failing because of some difficulty in the school; or structural factors rather than personal inadequacy may lead to a family being poor. In the first instance, our target for change would be some aspect of the school. In the second, we might try to work through the national organisation of FSU to bring about change that would alleviate the conditions of other families in this position. It is, of course, always much easier to define the referred client as the target for change, and bringing about change in some other system is frequently more time-consuming, or takes longer. We therefore try to do our utmost to improve the immediate condition of the referred client, while working for longer-term change.

For us, the unitary approach focuses attention on outcome, and this is critical. Although we may look for the cause or aetiology of a situation, it is never for its own sake, but in order to enable us to achieve the desired results. There is in our experience a danger that workers can use their particular theory of intervention without looking at results.

A study of the system described does provide a model that can inform intervention at the beginning, middle and closing stages of work. It is a model which enables workers to promote and order their social work knowledge, and relate this to planned intervention. It leads to a consideration of resources as well as needs, and encourages a consideration of public concern as well as private ills.

This model can lead to many different methods of work, but it would be wrong to equate multi-method work with the unitary approach. The chart on p. 32 has helped us to clarify the differences.

Values

A major pitfall in the unitary approach is that it can become pragmatic at the expense of good use of theory and clarity about values. Certain key values are implicit in using this unitary model: that clients may not be the only people who should change, and social workers may not be the best or only change agents, that social work should be based on an agreement between the change agent and the client.

It is possible to adopt different methods from different theoretical or value positions within a unitary model, e.g. a psychoanalytic approach with a particular client or a project aimed at producing change in a major social system. Often methods may be combined within an overall value position and it is helpful if the same model can be employed by social workers with different values. Difficulties arise when methods are combined by a worker without full consideration of whether there is a contradiction between the methods or theories that inform them and the values of the worker.

We have attempted to develop a congruence between values,

Figure 1. Differences between Unitary Approach and Multi-method Approach

	UNITARY APPROACH		MULTI-METHOD APPROACH

UNITARY APPROACH

(1) *Separates* { Client / Problem / Solution / Agency

(2) Removes need for medical model and *opposes pathology* as central interest of social worker.

(3) Puts focus on *contexts* of client, problem and solution.

(4) Is concerned with *interaction* between client, problem, and social environment.

(5) Ought to facilitate link between *private ills and public issues.*

(6) *It is common sense.* Start with problem or need and work towards solution. Do not start with workers' (agencies) problems or needs.

(7) Logically this leads to ways of *overcoming individualisation* of client and social worker. A consequence or necessary starting point is a *joint team approach* in which problems can be understood in their context, resources exploited to maximum, information gathered purposefully.

MULTI-METHOD APPROACH

(1) There is diversity and choice in terms of responses available to needs.

(2) Although no clear conceptualisation exists it seems to be *pragmatic* – if it works do it again.

(3) The basis of any overall conceptualisation would probably have to be *multi impact* theory – viz a range of responses hits at diverse targets and reinforces each other.

(4) It can easily accommodate the interest of a social worker and facilitate that worker staying within the boundaries of his own competence.

(5) You *don't need* much of a team to do it, just a collection of individuals with a variety of skills and interests.

(6) Preserves integrity of different methods.

(7) May help social workers not to develop too many symptoms of *schizophrenia* early in their career – but may defer rather than solve this difficulty.

theories and methods employed. A major value concerns our view of the clients with whom we work. Essentially, this is a belief in the dignity of the individual. We try to put this into practice by avoiding keeping secrets from clients, using open contracts more frequently, inviting clients to contribute to the work, and agreeing targets for change with them. Our clients have considerable difficulties at the time of referral but we neither view these difficulties as solely resulting from personal inadequacy, nor do we consider the individual or the family to be the appropriate target for change in all instances.

We have come to identify our broad goal as 'mature interdependence', within which we include the idea that family members need to find ways of helping each other without putting each other down, allied to ways of giving to and receiving from others in the community. However, this goal was initially dimly perceived, and the stages to reach it were not clearly identified. Groupwork has been most important in this respect. Clients have been able, through this medium, to identify common problems arising from national or local stresses rather than individual failure. Increased confidence has been achieved as clients have sought resources within themselves, and demanded resources from others. Furthermore they have increased their awareness of the extent and limitations of their own power, and have increased their participation in negotiations about decisions that affect their lives.

Origins of our Current Momentum

During the early and middle 1970s there were attempts by many agencies to move from the models that had previously informed social work practice. These models (as we caricature them) imply that the relationship between client and social worker alone was important in promoting change within the client. The baseline within the Unit had begun to depart from this model. We had carried out community work projects which had involved us in defining other agencies as targets for change and client groups as primary change agents. An emphasis on a private relationship between client and social worker was not the only model of work within the Unit: clients attended groups run by other workers and often visited the Unit to use its resources. We had a student unit located in the Unit, and students and recently qualified staff made us aware of new trends in social work thinking. Nevertheless, one-to-one work was the primary model that we employed, and it reflected a view of clients which we aimed to change. (In the early 1970s other agencies also perceived the Unit as the agency to which the most difficult 'multi-problem' families could be referred for long-term support and for a range of services including groupwork, casework and material aid.)

The pressures for change were various. There was a recognition that a major difficulty with this model was that it often failed to work; change of the order that workers thought necessary did not occur.

Relevant change that did occur took place in the first year, but files could remain open for over a decade. The Unit became an important part of some people's lives; it would take over the difficult task of paying bills, and was a comfortable warm place in which to sit and talk to others while using the Unit's sewing machine or cooker.

Another pitfall inherent in this model was the implicit notion that a family could move from dependence on the Unit to independence. However, it failed to take account of the forces which cause and maintain difficulties: neighbourhoods, families, or even agencies such as ourselves. Our attempt to elevate the dignity of the client was easily undermined by only focusing on the individual relationship.

There were other pressures for change within the Unit. A unit community-work project increased workers' awareness of community issues, and the networks that impinged on, or could be used for the benefit of our clients. A new Unit Organiser was appointed with community work and groupwork experience. In the spring of 1977, students on placement accurately described the Unit's style of work as a multi-method approach, and wrote a paper [5] which was included in a development plan written in 1977. [6] In this way, a movement towards a unitary approach became a formally agreed goal between staff and committee.

In what follows, we outline the stages we have reached in promoting changes in the organisational structure of our own Unit. This involves looking at team development issues. Later, we consider the impact of these changes on others, in particular the implications for our work with clients, and our liaison with other agencies.

Payoffs and Pitfalls of Initial Moves

It is fascinating to look back on that time. One of us remembers it as a time when we were clearer about what we did not like about the agency than what we really did value about the unitary approach which we were attempting to achieve. It feels now as if we were using the model more as a crutch than as a framework that truly informed practice. To use an analogy, some of our methods then were used somewhat as a drunk might use a lamppost; something to prop up his staggering path rather than something to illuminate it.

In 1977, we were unaware of the size of the task we had set ourselves when we decided to move towards a unitary approach; or the scale of the implications for our own internal organisation, or for other agencies. For example, Specht and Vickery [7] stress that one of the factors essential for the development of the unitary model is that 'workers are able to organise themselves for particular purposes into cohesive teams, and carry flexible roles'.

We return to this comment later. With hindsight, we appreciate that it carries with it some important lessons for the application of team working in achieving objectives. It also offers a way of avoiding a belief in teamwork for its own sake. An error was that we attempted simultaneously to develop the use of other action systems, and to tackle different target systems. The result was that we were developing the Unit annexe into a groupwork centre, beginning to work in patches, seeking to recruit a new team of social workers and beginning to use family therapy techniques without ever considering overall priorities. This all took place at a time when there was a major financial crisis in the Unit, which led to reduced staffing, and we were negotiating a different type of financial relationship with the social services department.

A pitfall of our attempting so much without an agreement on overall objectives, priorities and methods, was a lack of co-ordination in the changes that were taking place. One aspect of this was that some workers were concentrating on developing action systems in their patches, while others developed method skills. An emphasis on family therapy led to some workers temporarily abandoning attempts to move towards a unitary approach. Interestingly, these were the same workers who, as students on placement in the Unit, had been the main movers in raising the status of a unitary approach, and advocating its adoption. This seemed to be common among students, as we were told that all the students from this course had, for different reasons, abandoned the unitary approach when they became salaried social workers!

Fortunately, some of these difficulties contained the seeds of their own solutions. Family therapy pairs, although initially divisive, did lead to workers getting to know each other's work styles very well indeed, and this formed the beginning of a new measure of sharing in the Unit. This in turn led to an impetus to share with others through the medium of group supervision rather than the existing work review sessions.

We now had a number of meetings to discuss Unit policy in several different areas, and the weekly agendas for the Unit business meetings became very long indeed. We had moved from a pattern of individualism to a model where everyone participated in all decisions. Attendance at meetings declined, and much dissatisfaction was expressed.

Change followed when we recognised that we were trying to

devise a policy for a catchment area that was much too large for us to make any significant impact. One of the staff was given time to research the areas of greatest need. Following meetings with other agencies, we began to work in a much smaller catchment area in January 1979, which related to the results of the needs survey.

When two workers were due to leave, it was necessary to reallocate patches. A team member who had recently been on a course at the National Institute of Social Work suggested that this provided a good opportunity to work out the objectives we wished to achieve. It was generally accepted that this was a good idea, but not all members of staff were able to spend time on the matter.

A number of team members, however, expressed a commitment to working out an 'objectives tree' and attending all the meetings to do this: they became the 'core group'. Membership was open, so other team members did not feel excluded. Sheets of paper outlining our progress were left on the wall in the team meeting room, and we asked for comments. Unit staff who were not part of the core group did not feel excluded from the decision making, but did not feel obliged to attend all meetings. This method of a core group working on proposals which were then put to the larger staff group has since been used in other areas of work. The objectives tree (Fig. 2) outlines our general objectives, and the component objectives that derive from it.

The drawing of this tree was a demanding task for us but for the last year it has given us a clear basic answer to the question 'what are we doing?' One can either begin at the bottom of the tree asking 'why?', as one moves to each higher level, or begin at the top moving down and ask 'how?' For example, we ask *how* we 'promote policies and practices which lead to maximising the control families have over their own lives' we have identified three strategies, one of these being 'to develop families' skills in self help activity . . . ' . Conversely the answer to the question *why* we aim to 'develop families' skills in self-help activity . . . ' is that this is one strategy for promoting 'policies and practices which lead to maximising the control families have over their own lives'. Clearly we could have continued downwards through many stages. We have used it to review our time allocation between the three areas of activity given. Nevertheless, we are aware of internal inconsistencies and are, at present redrafting our objectives tree. We trust that this practitioners' illustration will encourage others to recognise and accept that good work which is far from perfect is of practical value!

We continued to have a large number of policy meetings about

Figure 2. Aims and Objectives of East Birmingham Family Service Unit — Summer 1979.

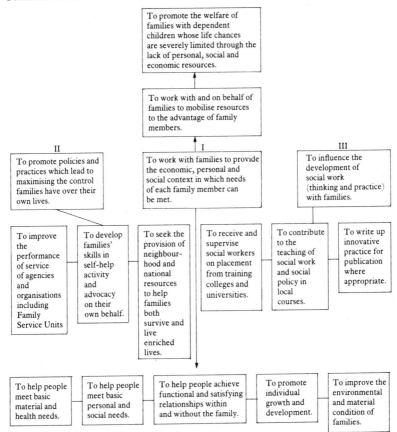

different issues and business meetings remained overloaded. In late 1979 we decided to call an embargo on policy meetings after having one final series of sessions to decide Unit priorities over the following six months. Following a reading of Townsend's *Up the Organisation* [8] one member of staff proposed strategies for streamlining the business meeting (see 'Techniques, Ideas and Methods' below).

There is a danger that in a move towards a unitary approach a team can become overloaded. There was a tendency for team members to develop target and action systems but at the same time maintain the same level of direct work with families. A great amount of overtime resulted. Following National Institute thinking and prompted by the clarity and purposefulness of the Specht and Vickery definition, a 'workaholics' self-help group of staff was established by some of the worst offenders and we began to move away from a Unit norm of working well above the required number of hours per week.

We also moved away from talking about caseloads and began thinking in terms of workloads. This acknowledged that it was appropriate for working time to be spent in ways other than direct contact with families. This is reflected in our weekly allocation meeting, as all work with families, groups or project work is allocated through the same process.

Most recently we have been piloting a method of recording that reflects our unitary perspective. The simplest form of this was the use of charts. For example:

Figure 3.

AIM	TARGET SYSTEM	CHANGE AGENT	ACTION SYSTEM
That John should attend school at least 4 times each week	John	Social worker	John EWO Social worker Parents Year Head at school
That the school positively accepts John's lack of a uniform	School	Social worker	Sympathetic Deputy Head Parents Social worker

We then listed the tasks that would contribute to achieving this aim. In the above example the tasks might be a visit to the school to reach agreement, or to agree methods of liaison between the agencies. Finally we indicated when we hoped to achieve the tasks. The latest scheme is more complex, in that it outlines the criteria or indicators which show that our aim has been achieved. Following the 'core group' principle, this pilot scheme is monitored by two staff members.

We are now increasing our use of clients as change agents for themselves and others. A single parent who is poor and may be lonely during the day may be in an ideal position to befriend and advise another single parent who has difficulty in managing on a low income and has built up large debts. The self-esteem of the helper is enhanced as he passes on to others skills that he has developed. The largest examples of this are our 'jamboree' sessions for clients in the Unit. When planning our groupwork programme we invited into the Unit the families with whom we were working and asked for their suggestions about groups we should run. We received a lot of positive feedback about this, and it has led to a marked improvement in attendance at groups. How often do we allow for our clients knowing what groupwork is appropriate for them? As our team has developed, we have become increasingly able to use each other as change agents. In this process, the use of the Unit centre has become more systematically planned and less haphazard.

An example of this kind of teamwork was with the P family. The father had long-standing mental health problems and at the beginning of our work spent almost the whole of the day in bed. Although he had received in-patient psychiatric treatment in the past, he had now been discharged from treatment and was diagnosed by his psychiatrist as no longer mentally ill. His wife, however, only related to him as if he were mentally ill, and gained satisfaction from complaining about him to anyone who visited as well as to the husband himself. As a result, his self-esteem was very low. A number of agencies had expressed concern about the baby who remained with the father while the mother was at work. The child was rarely fed during the day, in fact the father rarely lifted him from the pram.

We began our work with the twin aims of raising the father's self-esteem by increasing his activity and encouraging the development of a bond between father and son. We achieved this by encouraging the father to visit the Unit centre with his son. He found benefits in this as staff, students and other clients visiting the Unit made him welcome and commented positively on his son. Staff and students encouraged his efforts to play with his son and provide for his material needs. Mr P then acted as a volunteer for a social worker with another client, which served to raise his self-esteem still further.

We had thus created dependency on the Unit. Our next step was to prepare him for a different interdependence. Our use of other action systems increased. We worked with a psychiatrist to find sheltered employment in a training workshop. When this failed we employed him as an odd job man in the Unit for one hour a day. He signed a work contract agreeing to report to the Unit secretary, later the full-time volunteer, for work each day. A part-time place was offered to the baby at a nursery. Mr P stayed with the baby for one hour to benefit from encouragement and modelling by nursery staff and then came to the Unit to work. The health visitor continued to give advice on dietary requirements and general child care. When Mr P found a part-time job his work contract with the Unit was ended. Shortly after this his file was closed and responsibility for monitoring and encouraging further change passed to the health visitor and nursery.

Other Agencies: Some Thoughts on Managing the Boundaries

In this section we review the early failure of our first move towards greater openness to other people and organisations and look at the work intake and liaison channels we currently use. We also outline the patterns of collaboration we established.

We were and are seeking a considerable degree of adaptability. This continues to press us towards developing both a tighter team arrangement as an agency and a more open system that enables us to combine and collaborate with other systems serving the same catchment area. We have used contracts with both professional and client systems. This has been a major value to us in developing the kind of action systems we felt most appropriate.

The first moves towards a more active pattern of collaboration with other agencies were made in 1976. The catchment area was a two-mile radius from the Unit and was divided into five sections corresponding to the five social workers employed. Although this allowed us to increase knowledge of local agencies and to undertake some community-based programmes linking the work with families, family members in groups and other agencies, it was in fact divisive for the team. The goal of knowing and being known by other agencies was unobtainable in so large an area; and staff illness and changes added other obstacles which an agency with isolated workers was unable to overcome. Most significantly it tended to lead workers to choose between active participation with colleagues in the agency, or with other people on their patches. Success and difficulties on the patch were sometimes little known to colleagues. Furthermore the number of families known to us in most localities was too small to give the agency enough significance in each locality. Workers had little chance to develop the contacts that are the seedbed of collaborative action.

This disillusioned us, and led some workers to emphasise particular methods of approach as against using more generalist skills. Others aimed to be community based, to be receptive to the wider issues and to participate actively with other systems. We had failed to grasp fully the double message of our interpretation of the unitary approach: you must belong to a team and you must be able to work in participation with other systems. Another double message was an acceptance of the need both for individual professional development and for a focus on community needs. These double messages led us to step back. There was a considerable degree of staff conflict, which essentially lay in the failure to be realistic about objectives, the structure needed and the time scale required. We were setting new objectives in every aspect of the Unit's work. Pace was the major problem. Committee and management time were taken up with trying to resolve the financial crisis; changes in the national directorate meant that neither locally nor nationally were we confronted with the need for a team consultant. This we missed. [9] Below we outline some of the steps taken to resolve these difficulties.

In 1978 we set up a research project into the needs of the catchment area, in active association with the social services management and with help from their research specialists. This led to an agreement for a peculiarly shaped catchment area which related to need as shown by the social services and other statistics, and to bus routes. In future families would need no more than 35 minutes to come into the Unit. The new catchment area was about one third of the size of the earlier area. Advantages of working in the smaller area have included joint work with other agencies, such as school-based groups run jointly with teachers; the development of two Asian language and literacy classes run jointly with language tutors; family work with a Community Relations Council worker, with health visitors and with local authority social workers.

This has been accompanied by a greater readiness by other agencies to allow us to work with them. We have worked out clearer systems of liaison with the social services department concerning 'at risk' cases and statutory duties. We have also embarked on joint work with a community-based arts project, sponsorship of a drama project, active collaboration with one of the local church groups and closer ties with local councillors. We also began to make explicit contracts with our funders, notably the local authority, DHSS and industrial trusts. This package enabled us to return to the previous staffing level of Unit Organiser and nine social workers, including student training organiser and groupworker, as for a time shortage of funding had led us to leaving vacancies unfilled. Within the new catchment area no worker was operating in isolation from the rest of the team. Each worker was known both for his skills *and* community liaison responsibilities. Simultaneously we were appreciating anew that family issues have to be managed in step with relations between the family and other systems. Agencies communicated their image of us to clients, so that we found difficulty in discovering and changing assumptions about the services we could provide. By September 1979 we had improved patterns of liaison work with other agencies and groups, with four named workers as key workers for work intake on each patch. The groupworker initiated a major development by making our groupwork and other resources known to other agencies, and asking for group, individual and project referrals from them. Since these changes, referrals suggest that the image of our agency has changed. Certain types of requests for help are no longer seen as 'outlawed', and there is a growing recognition of the role we are trying to play in the community.

Projects tackled include our association with the development of a local youth club, a campaign for grants for school uniforms, and writing this paper. We also looked at areas which would involve sharing resources with other agencies. These developments each had to be worked out in detailed administrative terms so that records assisted all team members in advising other agencies of work programmes being offered. A new administrative secretary with a social science degree contributed greatly to this work.

Conclusion

We have discovered at a new level that just as anything that happens in a group or family system affects all other systems impinging on it, so with the Unit each internal development affects other local systems. A major management task for both team members and formally designated managers is to review how the boundaries of the agency are drawn and constantly to redraw them as work develops.

Techniques, Ideas and Methods we have found useful

1. Related to Negotiation of Roles of Team Members

Frequently in team meetings we find ourselves with jobs to allocate and roles to adjust. We have found in the past a reluctance in team members to say what they want from others and what they can offer to others. We insist that if people present their views they do this in as open a manner as possible. We now insist that people say exactly what they want. This principle is applied in twos, threes or full team meetings. It is interesting how often we avoid saying clearly just what it is we want and yet expect others to understand us.

Conflict is sometimes ascribed to individual team members when both the source and the solution of the conflict is confusion about roles. We are clear that roles need to be negotiated and renegotiated. Two sentence-completion frameworks that facilitate this are as follows: [10]

'In order to do your job better. . . .

(A)   (a) what do you want to see more of. . . .
     (b) What do you want to see the same of. . . .
     (c) What do you want to see less of. . . .

(B)   In working with you I most want you to find out about. . . .
    In working with you I least want you to find out about. . . .'

2. Meetings

We suspect that many moves towards a team approach fail because of inadequate skills in using meetings. We found great difficulties with this ourselves. In the Unit we have four types of meetings. During business meetings which are held weekly, events of the week are shared with one another and decisions are made about a range of different issues. Our weekly group supervision sessions are open to all team members and students in the agency and somebody from within or outside the agency presents a piece of work or an idea for group discussion. Work is allocated in short weekly meetings. We hold policy meetings at intervals of approximately six months in which we decide Unit priorities over the next six-month period.

Rules for Business Meetings

1.   There are two sections in our agenda for the Unit business meeting. All items are entered on the agenda for information *or* for decision.
2.   Information items either give the information or point to the source of the information. Such items are brief.
3.   Items for decision must come in proposal form, give the name of the proposer and the time required for the team to reach a decision. This is compatible with our policy of insisting that people say what they want from meetings.
4.   Any complex information has to be made available for people to read before the meeting.
5.   Items not posted on the agenda the day before the meeting are only discussed with the chairman's agreement. (The team of course, can challenge the chairman's ruling).
6.   Minutes indicate who is to do what and by when.

Group Supervision
Our weekly meetings last approximately one and a half hours. These have been crucial ways of learning about each other and about each other's skills and form an important bridge between our aims and how to achieve them. We have leaders for the group supervision sessions for three months at a time. Leaders are chosen by the group. There is always a group leader, a recently retired group leader to act as consultant and someone preparing to be the group leader by chairing business meetings. Information giving is kept to a minimum:

(a)   by focusing each session clearly
(b)   by circulating information beforehand
(c)   by the use of wall charts
(d)   if appropriate by the use of sculpting (see Note 1).

The beginning of the session is regarded as being vital for successful learning. We usually allocate five to ten minutes for playing a warm-up game. If a number of new team members join we may spend a whole session on team formation exercises. [11]

At the end of the session we usually ask for feedback on one good thing and one thing that could have been done better. We then do any planning necessary and allow ten minutes for a burning issue if it has been requested at the beginning of the meeting. We consider it very important to debrief after exercises such as role play work and sculpting. Techniques that we use include the 'group yell' (see Note 2) and giving our true name and identity clearly at the end of an exercise.

Allocation Meetings
Allocation meetings generally last for half an hour a week although occasionally we make special arrangements to have longer meetings. Allocation meetings enable us to share ideas about allocation of work and to make decisions. Information giving at the meeting is kept to a minimum by papers relating to the work to be allocated being placed in a folder at least the day before discussion. Supervisors are expected to attend but meetings are open to all. The allocation form is posted the week before the meeting and proposals are entered on it. These form the basis of the agenda. The form enables us to ensure that work is not commenced without clarity about who should supervise it. The form goes directly to the administrative officer after the meeting so there is no time lag between decisions being made and cards and files being established to represent that decision. Rules we

use in the allocation meetings are similar to those that we use in the business meeting.

Policy Meetings
We find that changes in one area of policy can often trigger off needs to change many other areas. We favour particular sessions for planning activity followed by a definite halt for six months, whilst decisions are worked out in practice. We have found it useful to review policy decisions briefly and ensure that team members are following through the policy decisions agreed. This takes place between meetings.

A key tool in the development of an agreed policy is the Objectives Tree (Fig. 2). This gives us a shared baseline of what we are seeking to attempt. It was very difficult to work out this objectives tree and it took about four months of meeting every three weeks to finalise it. We found it very tedious in the middle, but we suspect that there are no short cuts and that such an exercise will of necessity be very time consuming.

Developing Co-working Relationships
Many of the techniques we use were learned when the team attended a course in family therapy run by David Wilmot [10] and a course on social skills and personal problem solving run by Philip Priestley and James McGuire. [12]

Housedrawing Exercise The two workers hold the same pen and each tries to draw the house they would like to live in. After the exercise there is a feedback by each of the workers on how the exercise felt. Factors such as whether one of the workers seemed to dominate the exercise and the amount of co-operation and competition between workers are discussed.

Presenting Each Other's View of Work Each worker describes to the other their understanding of the other's views of work. There is a feedback on perceived inaccuracies.

Sentence Completion Sentence completion exercises are further methods used for workers to feedback to each other their work. They include the following:

(i)   What I like most about your work is. . .
        What I resent most about your work is. . .

(ii)   Five things I would like you to find out about my work
are. . . .

Five things I am concerned about you finding out about my
work are. . .

(iii)   Three things I want to contribute to the work are. . .

Three things I would like you to contribute are. . .

The Use of Tapes Interviews are frequently recorded. Co-workers
listen to the recording, and give feedback to each other and negotiate
any changes. It is preferable, but not essential, that the supervisor is
present at these sessions.

Immediate Post-Session Feedback Co-workers spend short periods of
time together after sessions for immediate feedback on their work
together.

Live Supervision Co-workers spend time planning a session with the
supervisor present as observer. Another alternative is for supervisors
to be present at sessions of family or material work.

Workload Management

We consider this to be extremely important in the Unit. When
individual workers become overloaded there are adverse effects for
the team, it is easy for difficulties to become individualised and the
amount of sharing declines. Some of the strategies to deal with this
problem, used on an individual and on a team basis are as follows:

Allocation Meeting The allocation meeting is aware of the workload
of the unit and of individual workers. Our aim, sometimes difficult to
achieve, is that new work is only taken on if there is team as well as
individual capacity.

Workloads We consider it vital that the overall workload rather than
the number of families that a worker is helping should be considered.
Significant work in the Unit, which requires allocation of time,
includes groupwork, staff and student supervision, duty periods and
liaison with other agencies within a patch. Particular workers may
also take responsibility for a section of Unit work.

Time Estimates Workers prepare estimates of the amount of time
required for each piece of work on the workload. Our aim, which is

often difficult to achieve, is that the weekly work of a full-time worker should not exceed 37½ hours.

Aims, methods or the pace of work may be adjusted if it is not possible to carry out planned work within the time limit immediately available.

Closing Work If a worker wishes to take on a new piece of work he is asked what work he intends to reduce or close in order to do this, unless it can be demonstrated that the workload is under 37½ hours per week.

Notes

(1) *Sculpting.* This is a technique frequently used in family therapy, in which members of the team represent a family, a group or sometimes an idea. [10]

(2) *Group Yell.* Everybody stands in a circle with arms linked. People begin by whispering, and gradually the volume is increased. Words whispered are sometimes one's own name, or sometimes something agreed in the whole group, perhaps a favourite brewery, or a political slogan.

References

1. A. Pincus and A. Minahan, *Social Work Practice Model and Method*, pp. 53–68. Peacock, Illinois, 1973.

2. D. Millard and G. Read, 'Teamwork and the Unitary Model in Probation and Aftercare Service'. *Teamwork in Probation* pp. 13–22. Midlands Regional Staff Development Office, 1979.

3. P. Leonard, Unpublished paper. University of Warwick, 1977.

4. T. Tierney, 'Differences between the Unitary Approach and Multi-method Approach.' Discussion at East Birmingham Family Service Unit, unpublished, 1979.

5. J. Rogers, 'The Unitary Approach'. Paper presented at East Birmingham Family Service Unit, unpublished, 1977.

6. Working Party on Devleopment, *The Development of Family Service Units*. Family Service Units, London, 1978.

7. H. Specht and A. Vickery, *Integrating Social Work Methods*, p. 240. Allen and Unwin, 1977.

8. R. Townsend, *Up the Organisation.* Coronet, 1971.

9. C. Fishwick, 'From Consultant to Facilitator and back in Probation and After Care Service'. *Teamwork in Probation*, pp. 47–60. Midlands Regional Staff Development Office, 1979.

10. D. Wilmot, 'Material Presented at Family Therapy Course' (unpublished). Birmingham FSU, 1978.

11. D. Brandes and H. Phillips, *Gamesters Handbook.* Tyneside Growth Centre, Newcastle, 1977.

12. P. Priestley, J. McGuire, D. Flegg, V. Hemsley and D. Welhar, *Social Skills and Personal Problem Solving: A Handbook of Methods.* Tavistock, 1978.

For Further Reading

H. Goldstein, *Social Work Practice: A Unitary Approach.* University of South Carolina, 1973.

P. Parsloe et al, *A Unitary Appraoch to Social Work Practice.* Hunter Ainsworth, Dundee, 1975.

A. Vickery, 'A Systems Approach to Social Work Intervention'. *British Journal of Social Work 4* (4), 1974. p. 389–404.

3. Supervision and Management in a Student Unit

Janet West

Introduction

Student supervision is intriguing, exciting, sometimes baffling, rarely dull. It has its pitfalls and its satisfactions. I often feel like a juggler whose art is to keep many precious balls on the move at the same time. What balls do I juggle and how do I keep them gyrating?

Let me present myself (the juggler) in the setting (agency) from which I operate. I am Janet, 42 years old, who entered social work in 1966 following training at Leicester University. After qualification I was a probation officer for ten years before moving to Leicester Family Service Unit (FSU) in 1976 as student training officer. Thus I had life experience, plus experience of student supervision and a thorough training in probation, mostly in rural Leicestershire. What was I to make of a student unit in a voluntary agency serving the city of Leicester? Almost all the external settings were different.[1]

I discovered that I was joining an organisation which has substantial commitments to student training and whose student training programmes were highly regarded. Here are some average annual FSU national figures:

	CQSW[2]	Other	Total
No. of students	164	29	193
No. of student days	9489	531	10,020
No. of courses worked with	86	6	92
No. of FSU supervisors	84	12	96

It is recommended that supervisors should have participated in a student supervision course, that they should *want* to supervise (essential!), that they should receive supervision on their supervision and that they should be qualified with at least two years' post-qualification experience.

Between 1968 and 1974, seven student training units were established by the Department of Health and Social Security

(DHSS) in Family Service Units. These were, in order of establishment, Oldham, Sheffield, Leicester, Birmingham, Newcastle, Bradford and Edinburgh. These units were 100 per cent DHSS-funded and were normally required to provide 800 student training days annually to professional student social workers. On average, sixty students a year have placements in FSU student units.

Leicester FSU

Although all twenty-two FSUs are different there are similarities, and I would like to describe the training unit at Leicester. Established in 1952, the Leicester Unit has, like all of us, changed and developed over the years. It comprises Unit Organiser, $3\frac{1}{2}$ social workers, a half-time volunteer organiser, groupworker, myself, two secretaries and part-time bookkeeper. On a council estate five miles away is the FSU Braunstone Neighbourhood Centre (Braunstone), which originated as a community work project and has expanded to include six weekly advice sessions for tenants who have problems with such things as welfare benefits, housing and education. A welfare rights worker, a community worker, part-time secretary and various tenants work there. This was a vigorous staff team into which to establish a student unit.

When I started at FSU, I had a lot of orientation to do in a short time because within three weeks a group of students was to arrive. I visited London and became acquainted with some other Units and the National Office staff. I picked up what I could from my new colleagues about their interests and expertise. I began to get the 'feel' of working in a voluntary agency located in what at that stage was a run-down area of a Midlands city. I discovered that the skills in the staff group complemented mine so that, to give the students an all-round learning experience, it seemed important to be able to draw on the expertise of my colleagues. In particular I decided that I would like to involve the groupworker and the advice centre worker into my programme. Accordingly a package of work experience for students was agreed by the professional staff and offered to courses.

Placement Experience available in the Student Training Unit

This splits into four components.

1. *Family work.* This is the core of the placement. It is done at some depth and the student is encouraged to try to effect realistic change given the families' circumstances and the time available. I take

overall responsibility and a range of social work methods is available, sometimes with the help of my colleagues. Students on concurrent placement (three days a week in the Unit) each have an average of four families at a time.

2. *Advice centre work at Braunstone.* An apt knowledge of welfare rights seems increasingly essential. It is a complex area and I decided that I would like my students to have the help of the advice centre worker. We arrange this by the student spending on average eight half-day sessions at the centre, first observing a more experienced worker conducting an advice session, then taking the session himself with the welfare rights worker available for back-up and oversight. If possible, he is given the opportunity to represent an applicant at a tribunal. The student has an orientation visit to the centre and is provided with information about the council estate, current benefit rates, and the agencies with which he may have to liaise. Additionally, the student observes how a small centre is run and the resources it provides for the estate. At Braunstone he is in the role of advice centre worker, which is a different perspective from that of social worker and which calls for sensitive preparation. The experience helps students to brush up their welfare rights knowledge as well as to develop their negotiating skills. It also gives practice in sharpening their interviewing techniques, as they have to get factual information about the clients' presenting problems in a short time. Not always easy!

3. *Groupwork.* This is another invaluable resource. We believe that in the right place, at the right time and applied in the right way, groupwork can be a precise instrument for effecting change. Students normally embark on a piece of defined groupwork, usually of between eight to ten sessions, with a co-worker, under the supervision of the groupworker. They are invited to set up, run and close the group and to evaluate its effectiveness, what they learnt from it and what groupwork skills they need to consolidate and expand.

4. *Other.* Students have the opportunity to follow some special interest. FSU is a flexible animal, not being bound by statutory obligations, and we have been able to provide interesting experiences. For example, students have spent time in the local psychiatric adolescent unit, in day nurseries and in courts.

Strengths and Problems of this Multi-method Approach and of using other Supervisors

The main strength is that I am not the students' sole fount of knowledge. It is increasingly apparent, as the social work task expands and the variety of methods (many of them effective if appropriately applied) increases, that no one supervisor can fully meet any one student's needs. My opinion is that within a team there is usually a range of knowledge and experience and that the group can often provide its own supervision if it is encouraged to do so; that is, if the team leader gives her approval. Therefore I encourage peer group consultation and enable students to discuss their work with other FSU workers. The aim is for the students to discover what is useful for themselves at that point in time, which is not always what I might be feeding them.

The strength of this argument can give birth to a problem. What happens when the student picks on a way of working that seems unsuitable? What happens when he is advised by someone without full knowledge of the circumstances? This is tricky ground for the supervisor but, provided she is in touch with all concerned, a difficulty that is not insuperable. Another problem can be the amount of liaison involved. It may seem quite a relief to hive off part of the supervisory responsibility but such delegation is only effective if I liaise with, and know what is affecting, my colleagues. Also I need to be able to feed to them any predicaments of the student that might hamper his effectiveness. Regular consultation with other supervising staff is essential.

Have you supervised in a goldfish bowl? That is how it feels sometimes. Supervision usually takes place privately but its strengths and shortcomings are available for all to see through the way the student approaches and discusses his work with other people. However, it is healthy that my work can be supplemented. After all, I am not omniscient!

My Accountability

Technically I have three masters, though I can add others. Where do my obligations lie? How do I make sense of this situation?

Being in a DHSS-funded Unit, I have to meet certain requirements. The Central Council for Education and Training in Social Work (CCETSW) is involved because, in the shape of a social work education adviser from the local office, together with a social work services officer from the regional DHSS office, it has an oversight function. DHSS needs to be satisfied that the 800 days are being reasonably accomplished and CCETSW looks at the professional content. In addition I work for FSU and thus have responsibilities to my Unit Organiser and local executive committee, as well as to national FSU management and policy makers. I also see myself as being responsible to the students and their courses; and I need credibility with the agencies whither the students return. Accountability to the families and their referrers is also important. If I expand the image of the juggler to incorporate aspects of Janus, you may understand! It works smoothly, provided my colleagues realise that at times I can have split allegiances.

Because local courses do not dovetail their placements so that there is a continuous flow of students in the field, there are times when the student training unit is stretched and times when it is comparatively slack. This has implications for work flow which by and large can be handled adequately, provided I maintain understanding contacts with people, usually outside the Unit, who supply me with referrals. It is impossible to expect the small Unit group to provide me with, and re-absorb, families, so I usually rely on outside sources such as social services departments, health visitors and the probation service. What can be more of a test is trying to prevent the permanent staff group from feeling swamped when there is a big, often lively, student group. In the early days, when the staff group was fragile for various reasons, balance was quite a problem and I found myself being the buffer and having to absorb tensions from both sides. Later the more established staff group was better able to assimilate the student peak times. However, I have some responsibility to ease the students into and out of the Unit with the least possible disruption to its permanent staff and to its ongoing work.

As well as informing the staff group about the rationale of the student group, I have to discuss with the students what sort of work the staff are doing. Sometimes the students try to emulate the staff, and this is not always appropriate. If we are not careful, there can be feelings on the students' part that they are second-class citizens. This is not true, but it may feel like that unless each understands the reasons for what the other is doing.

Other Reflections

Length of placement. I hold firm views on this. There are three main stages involved in social work intervention: entering and assessing the situation; working at defined areas to bring about change; termination. Whenever possible students should work through these three phases and, in the case of family work, this cannot properly be accomplished in less than six months, allowing for delays in picking up referrals and giving the student a second wave of referrals so that he can consolidate his learning. Added to that, my students will be working at Braunstone and with a group, so I recommend that the minimum stay in my unit should be six months, eight months being preferable. Also, on a practical level, it is more convenient to handle eight students at a hundred days each than thirteen students at sixty days.

Rationale for intake plans. As well as preferring long-placement students, I like to keep as even a flow of work as possible but I am largely in the hands of local courses here. What I have done is to evolve a basic pattern and I communicate to courses the vacancies I would like them to fill. The plan varies when course patterns change but at present it looks like this:

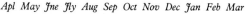

Apl May Jne Jly Aug Sep Oct Nov Dec Jan Feb Mar

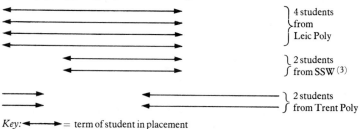

4 students from Leic Poly

2 students from SSW [3]

2 students from Trent Poly

Key: ◄───► = term of student in placement

It is helpful to have this baseline so that I can plan my own work and courses know where they stand as far as placements are concerned. Suffice it to say that I have not yet been undersubscribed;

Preferred type of student. I consider that my placement is best suited to the student who already has reasonable experience in social work or probation. It needs a mature student (many of the young students are amazingly mature), who has sufficient self-confidence to make use of the range of placement opportunities and who will not be thrown too easily by a sophisticated staff group and a multi-method approach. Problem students are acceptable, provided there is not more than one at a time and provided the needs of the majority are not jeopardised.

Supervision
Supervision is one of the most important balls that I have to juggle to

keep everything else in place. Supervision may sound somewhat complicated but in practice it seems to work well. Basically it is of two types: with the individual or with the student group. Individual supervision is tailored as far as possible to meet the student's needs. The group is used more for expanding awareness; much of the accountability and responsibility for supervision takes place in the individual sessions. The group can be whatever we want it to be. We use it for case discussion, experiential work, inviting specialist speakers and for looking at specific topics. I try to be flexible and to respond to what I perceive to be the needs of the group. Sometimes I ask the students to organise and chair the group. As well as professional input, I use the group for information-giving and other practical matters that can help the Unit's smooth functioning. It is often the numbers in the group that determine how we use it.

Timing varies; the group can meet weekly for $1\frac{1}{2}$ hours, but sometimes fortnightly. Individual supervision starts at $1\frac{1}{2}$ hours weekly (more in the first weeks), maybe moving to fortnightly supervision with consultation between sessions towards the end of the placement, when the student is probably also receiving weekly supervision from the group.

Preparation for individual and group supervision is as vital as it is in any other part of the social work task.

What Happens in the Training Unit?

In April four students, preferably second-year, arrive from the local polytechnic CQSW course. They will be in placement three days a week, except for twelve weeks in the summer when they will be full-time, and they have three weeks' holiday. If we follow them through their placement, this will demonstrate the things that I consider to be important.

Pre-placement Contact with the Course and Student

The course knows how many vacancies I have and the sort of student I consider suitable, and arrangements are made for prospective students to come for an exploratory visit. The aim is for them to meet me, to see the Unit and to find out about the placement. It is quite a complex placement and is not everybody's cup of tea, so some students withdraw. I ask the students to come together, as they will, after all, be working together and sharing themselves in the group.

Let us assume that five students come to see me. We talk about the placement, what they have heard, what they already know, what they would like to get out of it, what it can offer (not always the same). As well as factual information about the type of placement experience, I try to give them an impression of myself as a person. Also important to discuss is the implication of being in a student group, which is different from an individual placement. I take the prospective students on a tour of the building and leave them to chat with the students on placement. Then we meet to deal with further queries and I ask them to report their opinions about the placement to their tutor. I normally leave the course tutor to make the final selection of students, though on rare occasions I may intervene. For example, I may have a difficult student and do not want another at the same time; I may want to balance the sexes; the group may be engaged in something special into which newcomers would need to fit. Unless I want to have a hand in selection, I wait for the tutor to tell me who will be coming and to provide me with additional information that should include a potted biography, a synopsis of the student's social work experience and an assessment of his response to the course. A further pre-placement visit is not normally necessary but I write to the student, welcoming him to the placement, setting out the arrangements for the first days and giving diary dates.

Induction

Four students arrive in April when two students are nearing the end of the November/May placement. On their first day I ask the new students to arrive at about 10.30 a.m. so that we can have coffee and an introductory chat with existing students. I enjoy taking the students out to lunch, when established students and newcomers can get together over food and drink away from the Unit. We spend some time in the afternoon continuing the induction. During the first day I show students their desks, describe important bits of office routine such as where to look for messages and post, how the urn works, fire and safety precautions, meeting key people in the Unit. The second day we continue our induction and first family referrals are distributed. This takes place in the group, so that all students will know about all families, thus paying dividends when it comes to discussing work in the student group. Existing students help with the induction.

This is the check list I try to cover within the first week:

Induction Checklist

What is FSU? Differences from and links with statutory bodies.
Leicester FSU: staff and their work.
How the student unit fits into the main Unit.

The Unit — fire precautions; office routine, pigeon-holes, message book, movement sheet, coffee money, keys; security of the building; minibuses, insurance and booking procedures; Unit meetings and arrangements for staff supervision.

My background, orientation, workload, accountability.

Non-accidental injury procedures.

Family work in FSU.

Initial contacts with the groupworker and Braunstone.

Student's expectations of placement; student's workload; student assessment procedures.

Tutor visits.

Recording.

Use of block parts of the placement.

Supervision – group/individual.

Transference issues, e.g. previous placement, previous fieldwork, previous supervision.

Each student is provided with a basic information file that includes:
A diary.

The Unit's family work assessment outlines.

Non-accidental injury documentation – an extract from the Leicestershire Area Review Committee's guidelines, the British Association of Social Workers' Code of Practice and the Unit's guidelines.

List of Unit staff's names and trades.

Paper for recording, notes, etc.

Child Poverty Action Group Handbook on Welfare Benefits, for which the student pays.

A sheet of useful information about office procedure.

Background articles about FSU and a copy of the Unit's latest annual report.

First Stages of the Placement
The students need time to settle in and find their feet but also need sufficient structure to feel contained. Giving students time is achieved fairly easily by making sure that their diaries are not crammed with appointments. Sufficient space is vital at the beginning of a placement because the student needs to absorb many things, not just with his head but with his senses, feelings and intuition. Apart from acquiring factual information, much processing of impressions is taking place. The student is grappling with what it is like to be back in a fieldwork agency. Students often come on placement having been de-skilled to some extent by their courses. That is not to say that

courses deliberately set out to hamper their students. What seems to happen is that students pick up new ideas which challenge their earlier ways of working. Thus the student queries his previous effectiveness and rationale for being a social worker, so he comes on placement wondering who he is now. He is not the social worker whom he knew previously, neither does he know how (or whether) he can function with half-digested but untried ideas, facts and feelings that the course has generated. Also he is on placement: his work and he are being assessed, his records will be scrutinised. If this is not enough, he has to contend with working in a voluntary agency. What are the differences? What is it like not to have statutory over-tones? All this can be bewildering, so students tend to find the first days tiring and I make it easy for them to arrive late and go home early.

The students usually quickly identify as a student group. Integration with the staff group is slower, though staff and students make individual and often close links. There is usually a bit of 'them' and 'us'. Should there be? Can it be avoided?

Introduction to Family Work

Family work runs throughout the placement and one or two referrals each are allocated within the first days. The induction included an exploration of how the students might perceive the differences between their previous experiences and their FSU placement, how they might feel diffident about interviewing again and how I accept that their skills might decrease for a while. We look at the need for precision in problem definition, the advantages of short-term work, how a period of assessment is useful (coupled with 'treatment' of course) followed by a sequence of planned intervention, how mistakes are permissible. Do we not usually learn from our mistakes? I have. Mistakes can be valuable. The integrity of professional social work students usually precludes the worst blunders and errors are retrievable. So the student will be put on the road of assessment, diagnosis and treatment. He will be encouraged to try methods of work not previously attempted (which implies that he needs to be secure in the supervisory and placement setting); I see the placement as opening new windows as well as consolidating existing skills.

Recording

The student is introduced to agency files. At the beginning of the placement I ask for running records of all contacts on behalf of the family and I request that interviews be written up as fully as possible.

This is for two reasons, one of them selfish. I find it helpful to have descriptive material about the family in the early stages, as it is unlikely that I shall have met them. A descriptive record, in addition to hearing the student talk about the family, gives me a feeling and impressionistic information that helps me to 'fix' that family in my mind and to recall its circumstances in some detail (a useful asset when I am supervising work with over thirty families). Secondly, most students find it helpful to be able to explore the interview by writing it up in detail.

Students are given the following guidance about recording:

1. It should be done and it should be kept up to date.
2. Each interview should be recorded in three main sections:

(a) *Aim of interview.* This means that the student needs to think beforehand about its purposes. If the interview deflects from the aim, so be it; there are often good reasons. If not, we can explore why.

(b) *What happened in the interview.* This is usually detailed and students tend to write it chronologically or according to the various points raised.

(c) *What happens next?* What is the next stage of intervention? What else will the student do? For instance, does he need to contact DHSS, consult another agency, or visit the school? As the placement progresses, the student will be asked to streamline his recording. If the tape recorder is a mystery, he will be encouraged to become familiar with its use.

Occasionally I ask for process recording, using it when there is a point of difficulty, perhaps blockage, in some interaction. Usually I suggest process recording around a specific issue rather than of a whole session. I am not persuaded that process recording is ideally used at the beginning of a placement and find some corroboration for this in Bertha Reynolds' book. [4]

Introduction to Braunstone and Groupwork

Students are given theoretical and factual background by me and the specialist workers to enable them to begin to function in these settings. I take responsibility for the overall co-ordination of their experiences and for ensuring that the students' workload is as equable as possible. Usually students will have finished at Braunstone before beginning in the groupwork, or vice versa.

Further Thoughts on Supervision

For me and for the student there is the delicate art of tuning in to each other so that we can attempt to form a productive relationship. I am myself and the student is himself. There can be basic differences in these two selves and it is useful to know what they are. I bear in mind three things:

1. Does the student work mainly intuitively, with his feelings, with his head, or practically through his senses? Is he opposite to me or similar?
2. Does he learn inductively or deductively (i.e. doing and then theorising, or theorising before doing)? How do I learn?
3. Is he basically extrovert or introvert?

There is no 'right' answer but there are important variables. For instance, if I have a student who learns best by reading textbooks and theorising as a prelude to his interviews, I would do him a disservice if I encouraged him to go into the interview without much fore-thought and to react on the spot to what his feelings told him. Both these approaches are valid (though social work training might jib at the second?). A fuller explanation of these three points can be found in West. [5]

Also I need to know about his previous supervisory experience. Was it rich or was it non-existent? Did the student make the running or was he 'done to'? What are the transference issues we might have to look for?

Something that I suspect can be overlooked is the supervisor discussing with the student what would be the most helpful style of conducting the sessions. Who sets the agenda? Is supervision based on the student's current work or on the pre-selected topics? Does the supervisor require recording beforehand? Is she likely to take a didactic or a reflective role? Is punctuality expected and what are the time boundaries? Does the supervisor allow interruptions? Will supervision be regular or ad hoc? If ad hoc, at whose behest? Is the supervisor available outside sessions? It is important that this type of issue is clarified, otherwise I have found that there is a danger that neither person gets what they expected from the session, with resultant confusion.

Enter the College Tutor

There is a need to clarify the role and expectations of the college tutor. Normally the tutor visits us in the early stages of the place-ment. Although some of this will have been established in the pre-placement contact, we need to confirm what the student's learning needs are thought to be, what type of work experience can best meet them, what weaknesses and gaps have been identified that we can remedy, what is the student's performance in the college setting. Also it should be made explicit how the supervisor, tutor and student view their roles.

I maintain (against what has tended to be current practice) that supervisor and tutor as a twosome should have the right to discuss the student rather than the tradition that the student can only be discussed in the threesome. After all, supervisor and student meet together (the tutor's ears may burn at times!) and student and tutor have their tutorials (when the failings of the supervisor may be aired), so why not tutor and supervisor? I feel it is essential that I have the right to go to the tutor, but this would normally be with the student's knowledge. There was one occasion when I had a student whose performance fell – quite dramatically – below my expectations. Was I at fault? Was there something I had not been told? I needed to check my feelings with the tutor before discussing my observations with the student. It transpired that there was a wealth of disturbing material with which I had not been acquainted and the fact that I discovered it and was then able to use it as illustrative material with the student, helped us untangle this unhappily knotted situation. I doubt whether I could have handled it as effectively had I tried to do all the unravelling in the threesome.

Therefore I suggest that the purpose of tutor visits should be made explicit and that we should have an understanding of the professional relationships within the threesome. At best tutor visits can be a joyous stimulation; at worst a mundane occurrence. On long placements tutors can usefully keep in touch with their students' practical work by no less than three visits, usually at the beginning, middle (interim assessment time) and end. Tutor visits to a student unit supervisor when she has a lot of students can be time-consuming and need careful timetabling. Sometimes I advise tutors when it is convenient for them to come, thus obviating 'tutor swoops' when they all try to flock in on one week!

Supervisor's Notes
I try to keep tabs on the content of supervision sessions, student groups and tutor visits by jotting down brief notes in the student's files. These are intended to ensure that I do not forget what I said I would do and to remind me of what has happened. The file is open to the individual student, (though my squiggly writing is probably a deterrent!). Whatever the occasion, a reminder of the previous session is a good prelude to the next and I have found it particularly useful with tutor visits.

Weak Students

It is imperative that the supervisor should discuss with the student at the earliest opportunity any doubts she may have about his performance. It makes good practice to let the student establish himself in the Unit, but it is usually possible to see quite early on if the student is underfunctioning. I find that a frank discussion, using the student's work as illustration of what may be going wrong, brings a good deal of relief for the student, who almost always knows that all is not well. Once the difficulty is admitted (the tutor probably needs to be informed or involved at this stage), it can be worked on. Although I have experience in psychological counselling, I do not consider it appropriate to counsel the student myself. I have a firm rule that if the difficulty is caused by personal problems, I suggest that the student refer himself to an appropriate source for help, such as doctor, marriage guidance counsellor, psychological counsellor, masseuse. The student has an inner momentum that makes him want to get 'well' and he usually makes full use of such help. In one instance, I gave a student six weeks' leave of absence; during that time he clarified many of his inner problems and came back a more relaxed and better worker. Conversely, if the student were getting into difficulties because of lack of technique or poor theoretical knowledge, I would do what I could to remedy that. In one case I offered a student an extra weekly session, to be used as he liked, in an attempt to broaden the social work base that I felt to be severely lacking.

I would consider it extremely bad practice if I left until the evaluation session any doubts I may have about the student's ability as a social worker. At that stage it is almost too late to work constructively, the student will be shocked and angry if no intimation has been given beforehand, and the whole thing could become an unnecessarily difficult mess.

The Middle Phase

It is now June and the placement is well under way. We are working in a group and individual supervision sessions are prospering. However, nothing stays the same for long and we are to enter a phase of change. Two new students arrive in July and with all the students (and hopefully myself) having three weeks' holiday, we are in for a period of disruption.

Integration of New Students

For the Poly students it is now interim assessment time, which seems to me to be a more important event than the final assessment. Ideally, assessment should be continuous and nothing should arise in the assessment sessions that is not already known to student and supervisor. How easily one falls short of the ideal! If courses do not have formal interim assessment procedures, I tell them what I consider to be their shortcomings in this respect and, provided the student agrees, at about the half-way stage I institute a formal interim assessment, using the end-of-placement guidelines if there are no specific interim assessment requirements. The assessment can be done in several ways:

1. I draft the assessment, which is discussed with the student.
2. The student drafts the assessment for discussion with me. This often highlights interesting material of which I was not fully aware.
3. Student and supervisor meet for discussion, then either drafts the assessment which is then discussed.

These days, it is frowned upon for the supervisor to complete the document without recourse to the student and student participation is welcomed. I usually adopt the third alternative (though find there are strengths for certain students in the second), feeling it helpful to come to the discussion knowing what I want to contribute and being prepared to listen to the student. What happens if student and supervisor differ on certain points? Sometimes it is possible to compromise, sometimes not. When agreement is impossible I reserve the right to say what I want, giving the student the right to add a rider explaining his perception.

Consolidation and Summer Holidays

Students are taking stock of their social work intervention and are usually entering a deeper, often more challenging, stage. They are also consolidating some of the things they learnt at the beginning of the placement and are working for the rest of the placement on the objectives identified in the interim assessment. I will have tried to work with the student group so that they trust one another and know each other's work because, where possible, I ask them to cover for each other's holidays.

The pacing of work is important. Family work is usually task-focused to some extent, so I get the students to calculate how many weeks they and the family have before the next holiday (or end of the placement) so that we can aim for reasonable targets. It is important that families are not left on too tense a note when the student goes away or they may not be able to contain the holiday period without distress. If properly handled, we usually find that the families come through students' holidays without undue trauma and, if interviews have been sensitively paced, the student is often able to pick up more-or-less where he left off.

I like holidays too! It goes without saying that there is hardly ever a 'right' time to take a holiday, but provided students know in advance that I am going away and what arrangements will be made for my absence, problems are usually minimal. Normally I arrange, with the students' consent, that they supervise each other, often in the student group, but certain work may be discussed in pairs or trios. There are always professional staff in the Unit whom the students can consult but they work hard by themselves and find that they have had a rewarding experience.

Final Phase

In September we enter the final phase of the placement. Involvement with families and groups continues vigorously but will be phased out so that, a week prior to the end of the placement, client contact is terminated with the family work being closed or transferred to other workers in FSU or outside agencies. The students are beginning to see beyond the Unit towards the next part of their lives, be it a continuation of the course or returning to their jobs. In supervision and in the group I try to help them to look at the next stage and I know that some students need to withdraw from the placement to some extent to free themselves to prepare for the future. Students are usually ready to progress and this is essential. I would have failed if at the end of the placement the student were still tied to my or the Unit's apron-strings.

Final Asssessment

We may prepare the final assessment the same way as the interim assessment or we may do it differently. The final assessment is on quite a big scale because this is where the student's workload and all his placement experiences are demonstrated. I take responsibility for responding to the course guidelines and the specialist work is acknowledged in appendices. Appendix 1 is the student's synopsis of his total work experience. The groupworker and student provide an Appendix 2. The student produces a self-assessment of his welfare rights experience at Braunstone (the welfare rights worker prefers not to assess formally, although she supervises and teaches him) in an Appendix 3. If anything else has been attempted such as family therapy with one of the social workers, this is included in an

Appendix 4. As a supervisor, I consider that I have the right to recommend whether the student passes or fails the placement.

Final Days
It is December and I need to check that the necessary things have been done, that files are complete, case notes up to date, closing or transfer summaries satisfactorily written on families, that the families know that the student is leaving and what arrangements, if appropriate, are being made for transfer. Additionally I ensure that students hand in their Unit keys, have paid their coffee money, have returned borrowed books, and have left me with a contact address in case of any immediate queries and so that I can send them a questionnaire relating to the usefulness of the placement on their return to the field.

During the last days we usually have a social function, either a lunchtime get-together in the Unit or a meal out.

But the student unit is not dead because in November two new students arrived from Trent Poly. Thus the cycle continues.

Some Other Important Balls to Juggle
There are other aspects to my work that have not yet found space but which are important.

Contact with Courses and Social Work Development
As well as links with students' tutors, there is scope for productive contact with courses. Experienced supervisors will be familiar with the examples: helping courses to interview prospective CQSW students; sitting on committees and formal boards; taking part in induction courses; participating in advisory groups; joining CCETSW reviews. Some supervisors contribute to course teaching. It is important to keep this portion of my work in balance and I restrict such involvement to my local courses, with a few exceptions. Otherwise I could always be at meetings. I consider that I am a useful link between practical fieldwork and academic theory and therefore have a pertinent contribution to make in the academic setting.

As well as taking from DHSS and CCETSW, I have the opportunity to contribute to some of their deliberations on policy and professional matters. It is important that there should be a two-way flow and that I, as a student unit supervisor, take some initiatives and accept some responsibility for trying to clarify the role and purpose of social work training.

Supervisor's Needs, Frustrations and Satisfactions
My needs should not be overlooked. 'Giving' to students can be stimulating but it can be wearing and the sensitive supervisor knows that she herself needs to receive some 'giving'. For me important areas are to have supervision, to meet other unit supervisors, to expand my own horizons professionally and personally, and to make sure that I get regular care and attention from someone whom I can respect. It is imperative that I should want to supervise because if my supervision becomes dreary and routine, then students and clients may suffer a disservice.

The work has its share of frustrations, though is amply helped by students who are usually full of enthusiasm. The student workload can be unbalanced, with fat times and lean times according to the vagaries of courses. Having three (or more) masters demands careful adjustments. I can put much energy into a student who disappears. The students sometimes do work that I would like to try myself. They may do something that I consider inappropriate: sometimes they are right, in which case I have to look at myself; sometimes they are not right, in which case we try to improve the situation.

The job, however, has its rewards and these can be many and bountiful: I enjoy the comparative freedom I have within the bounds of my professional responsibilities. I rejoice when I see students develop professionally and personally. It is satisfying to be able to contribute at a number of levels to effective social work practice in the future. Above all, it is creative interaction with people, be they student, client or colleague, that gives the deepest satisfactions and sense of fulfilment.

Notes and References

1. 'Unit' designates Leicester Family Service Unit, whereas 'unit' is used for the student training unit within the 'Unit'. The student is referred to as 'he' and the supervisor as 'she'.

2. Certificate of Qualification in Social Work awarded by the Central Council for Education and Training in Social Work in conjunction with the academic bodies.

3. Leicester University School of Social Work.

4. B. C. Reynolds, *Learning and Teaching in the Practice of Social Work*, p.239. Russell, New York, 1965.

5. J. C. West, 'Student, Supervisor and Personality Type'. Unpublished paper.

4. Supervision in Groupwork

Pam Donnellan

'I learned that another part of a supervisor's skills as far as the workers are concerned, is to know all the answers. I was able to get out of this very easily. I discovered that when a worker asks a question, the best thing to do is to immediately ask what she thinks. While the worker is figuring out the answer to her own question, (this is known as growth and development) the supervisor quickly tries to figure it out also . . . In the event that neither the worker nor the supervisor succeeds in coming up with a useful thought, the supervisor can look wise, and suggest that they think about it, and discuss it further next time . . . giving the supervisor plenty of time to look up the subject, and leaving the worker with the feeling the the supervisor is giving great weight to her question.' [1]

Many readers will recognise the 'one good question deserves another' supervisory game, and may know several more. I hope during the course of this chapter to look in a more positive way at the supervisory role in relation to social groupwork, as it has developed in the Leicester Family Service Unit.

The establishment of a groupwork post in the Unit is some indication of the value placed on this method of intervention by the Unit, although this does not appear to be a shared value in the area, as I know of no other similar post in the social work agencies in Leicestershire. The main focus of the caseworkers in the Unit is family therapy, but they can and do run groups other than family groups. There are close links with the student training unit, which is described in Chapter 3. All students have the opportunity and expectation of some groupwork experience. My role is that of a specialist practitioner offering supervision to both caseworkers and students running groups, and I have overall responsibility for the development of groupwork practice in the Unit. The Unit attempts to offer a city-wide service, with the majority of clients being referred from other agencies.

Two years' experience in this role has led me to the following conclusions: First, that social work clients rarely refer themselves for, or expect to receive, groupwork help. Notable exceptions to this are recognised groups such as 'Alcoholics Anonymous' and 'Weight Watchers'. Second, that social workers rarely consider groupwork techniques of intervention seriously. Recognition of these two facts has led to a widening of the supervisory role from its traditional 'how' context, i.e. how to run a successful group and how to realise workers' potential, into the areas of 'why' and 'what', i.e. why groups? and what groups work best?

I propose to make some general observations about groupwork practice from a fieldwork supervisor's perspective, before looking in detail at the principles and practice of that supervision.

The Place of Groupwork in Practice

Most social workers would be able to provide a theoretical justification for some types of social groupwork as an appropriate intervention in a given social situation. Why then, is its development in social work agencies on an occasional and ad hoc basis, often depending on the commitment and enthusiasm of one or two workers? Part of the answer lies with the agencies, and part with the training courses.

If we consider the development of social services departments, it is possible to see that the role restraints operating on social workers, the expectations of service delivery, and the organisation of work into 'caseloads' can prevent the practice of groupwork being seen as an integral part of the work. There is also the question of social workers' attitudes and feelings towards groupwork. Parsloe [2] found that social workers believed themselves to be inadequately trained, and that those who had received social work training found groupwork more difficult than untrained workers. Parsloe puts forward the view that all training seemed to do in relation to groupwork was to 'alert people to its problems without giving them sufficient experience to feel that they can handle them'.

This certainly confirms my experience with students arriving at the Unit on placement. Their comments about course teaching on groupwork often reflect a bewildering mixture of theoretical (didactic) and experimental learning which appears only to have deified groupwork into the realms of the mystical. Most workers have at best ambivalent attitudes towards groupwork. They see it as threatening: groups break people down – damage people – can't put them back together. The power of group pressure, often experienced by many in adolescence, makes students feel that running a group, and enabling a group to work at a given task, is too daunting a venture. Individual casework and family work *seem* easier, and are generally carried out in a less public arena, so that fear of one's weaknesses being exposed is less severe. Leadership skills and the use of authority, are central issues in groupwork, and cannot be avoided as can often happen in one-to-one casework. To run groups effectively requires hard work, and a high level of commitment.

Often social workers receive little recognition for their groupwork by the agency, nor overt support from their colleagues. Perhaps the way we have approached groupwork at Leicester Family Service Unit is a way of reducing some of the difficulties.

Through supervision, progress towards achieving the aims of the agency can be monitored and the individuals concerned with those aims are helped to use their abilities and develop their potential to the full. This is a rather dry and static definition of supervision. The dynamics of the personal transactions involved are varied and complex.

The responsibility of supervisors to monitor work, so that aims and standards set by the agency are met, is often seen as essential by supervisors; and irrelevant, or at times even harmful, by the recipients who are more concerned with the degree of help and support that they receive. A measure of constructive criticism is allowed, but the 'consultative' model is often seen as safer and more acceptable than the 'supervisory' model. The art of effective supervision appears to lie in achieving a balance between the two. This often feels to the supervisor like trying to walk a tightrope, for our attempt to achieve objectivity depends on a consensus of opinion about the knowledge and skills within the profession, which is in itself elusive. As supervision progresses, so agreed frameworks and shared assumptions about social work are developed, and more time can be spent on the core concern of increasing interpersonal skills and professional expertise.

It can be useful to look at the acquisition of knowledge and skills in groupwork in terms of three distinct perspectives — knowing, feeling and doing. Knowing is taken in its educative, cognitive sense. Feeling is related to experiential learning by being a group member. Doing relates to the learning that takes place by practising the skills in simulation exercises, or direct experience of running groups.

Knowing. What do potential groupworkers know about groups? Students on placement with us have often had very little theoretical input. Psychodynamic principles such as Bion's 'basic assumptions' have often been taught in a vacuum, and are seen to have little real value. So myths abound. 'It is all about selection of group members', said one student. 'We once spent six months in the office trying to work out elaborate criteria for group selection, by which time our colleagues could not find anyone suitable to refer.' Sometimes students arrive on placement before they have reached the groupwork teaching on the course. 'Oh, we don't do groups till next year!' Often the common base of groupwork knowledge is split between different parts of the course. For example, residential work involves a knowledge of group processes and dynamics, as do studies of organisational behaviour and management theories. The need for some theoretical framework is often very apparent.

Feeling. What do potential groupworkers feel about groups, and about their ability to lead one? 'We had this day on the course when a bloke came and made us all play stupid games — then he split us all up into groups of eight, and we had to sit in a room and talk about how we felt, and what was happening — I just went home. It seemed senseless to me.' 'I went away to a weekend on group dynamics run by an eastern religious group, but they locked us up and didn't give us enough to eat — so I rang a friend, and ran away in the middle of the night.' 'This chap went to do some groupwork in Borstal, and the first week he demonstrated a trust game. He ran at a wall, and the boys were meant to stop him, but they all moved away, and he broke his nose on the wall.'

Our fears, fantasies and assumptions about groupwork need to be shared before we can work with groups in a positive way. Workers often feel they possess few personal skills in relation to groupwork, and lack basic confidence in their ability. In fact workers have many skills and resources which need to be made explicit.

Doing. What previous experience have workers gained? 'I helped to run an intermediate treatment group once — but I didn't really know what it was all about or what I was supposed to be doing.' 'I helped a group once. This guy Tom ran it, or thought he was in charge, but the other two social workers thought they should have an equal say — anyway it didn't last long, because the kids started to drop away, and soon there weren't enough coming.'

Despite the experiences quoted above, most social workers have far more experience of groups than they realise, but have not recognised its relevance. The group dynamics observable on their social work courses, as well as membership of leisure groups, school and family groups provides a wealth of untapped knowledge.

It also happens that social workers are not encouraged to 'process' their group experience, so that its value and relevance is understood and is retained for the future. All too often, social workers have been involved in groups that lacked explicit leadership and/or had no supervision or consultation built in. It is paradoxical that many social workers inexperienced in groupwork would not expect to be offered specific supervision if they ran a group, rather feeling that they would 'have to get on with it and prove themselves', whereas no self-respecting experienced groupworker would contemplate running a group without demanding or seeking out appropriate consultation.

Fieldwork Training in Groupwork

In this and the following sections, I shall describe the methods of training and supervision which I use both with students on placement and with social work staff learning groupwork skills. I shall use the term 'students' throughout, as describing the position of social workers and students in relation to groupwork.

I begin supervision by looking with the students at the three areas of knowing, feeling and doing outlined above. I prefer to do this as a group exercise, so that all the students begin to recognise not only where they stand in relation to groupwork, but where each other stands; so that we are all, hopefully, beginning to explore myths, and become more reality-based in our work. My starting point is that *groupwork can be an exciting and effective method of intervention. It is within the capabilities of most people.*

A simple questionnaire or paper and pencil exercise can explore where each student is in terms of knowing, feeling and doing. The questionnaire I use is the following:

Knowing
1. What experience in groupwork do you have?
   as (a) group member
      (b) group leader
2. What teaching/learning in groupwork have you received?

Feeling
3. List six things you enjoy in life.

Doing
4. List three strengths you possess as a social worker.
5. List three weaknesses you feel you have as a social worker.
6. Locate yourself as a social worker on these two continuums

   Passive ◄─────────────────► Active
   Permissive ◄─────────────────► Directive

This can be shared in pairs, and then followed by a general discussion of what assumptions, fact and fears have emerged. I find that this type of exercise helps to establish a relaxed working alliance with some of the negative tension resolved. The gap between what people do and what they say they do is beginning to be reduced. The general discussion allows people to recognise experience in related group situations thay may previously have dismissed. It helps me to know what knowledge students have acquired, and what future learning may be valuable.

If lack of confidence is a common feature, I feel it is important to build on students' strengths rather than confuse them further by detailed theorising about groupwork, only leading to further mystification.

In beginning to approach the why? and what? questions – why run groups? what sort of groups work best? – I find a simulation exercise most useful. My starting point is that groups are devised as an appropriate response to a social situation. I divide the students into pairs or threes, and armed with their previously completed questionnaires, as resources they possess as workers, they devise a groupwork response to a given situation.

Simulation Exercise
(normal time allowed, 45 minutes)

Social situation. There is some concern about a group of adolescents, several of whom are known to the agency, living on a local council estate. There is a high rate of truancy, and concern about increasing vandalism.

This statement, given to all participants, is intentionally vague in order to represent the sort of comments heard in an agency, which can lead to the formation of groups.

During the exercise I act as a resources person, possessing all relevant knowledge about the agency and the given social situation. The pairs or threesomes work as independent subgroups, and can consult me at any time for information, and for higher management decision making.

At the end of the time each subgroup presents its proposals to the whole group.

I have used this exercise with students both on placement and in college, and I find it produces outlines of varied and imaginative schemes. Social workers can see that there can be several different and valid approaches to any particular problem; that working together can be creatively productive and also enjoyable; that they gain confidence in looking at new ways of working. From the brief outline of schemes devised, the group can then begin to look at appropriate frameworks, both theoretical and practical, for planning and running soundly based effective groups. This then is the second stage that I move on to in supervision.

Planning Groups
The basic framework for planning which I use is taken from the work of Douglas: [3]

>Group purpose
>Group type
>Group methods to be used
>Theoretical base

followed by more structural concepts: time, place, duration, frequency, membership, contract, leadership, recording, liaison, supervision. Students can begin to analyse their proposals in the simulation exercise according to the above framework, especially the first four related elements.

Group purpose or aims. Being specific about the purpose of a group in the planning stage causes students great difficulty. Too often, muddled generalisations are offered. Usually the aims are unrealistic, expecting greater change or growth than can be hoped for. Helping students to set achievable aims in their work is not restricted to groupwork practice. The difficulty is due in part, I feel, to the logical progression from stated aims to evaluating the outcome. Students often associate evaluation of their work in success or failure terms, which can inhibit the setting of specific goals. If evaluation is seen more in terms of a development process, this can help students to feel less anxious and less 'on trial'.

A basic typology of groups can aid clear thinking and help students to make sense of the term 'groupwork'.

>Leisure groups
>Educative groups
>Social work groups — supportive orientation
>   — supportive/change orientation
>Psychotherapy groups

The categories are not mutually exclusive, and it is possible for groups of one type to contain elements of another. For example, a recent social skills training group for mentally handicapped adults contained several important educative elements.

The methods used in groups to achieve the stated aims encompass a wide range, from discussions, role playing, psychodrama, crafts, physical activities and many more. It is important for students to become familiar with a wide range of techniques, and to develop practical experience in their application. For example, if students are keen to use games, then a group supervision session can be focused on this, with each worker in turn leading the group. They can then gain some practical skills in introducing games to a group, and assessing their value through feedback from their colleagues. A useful compendium of games can be found in *The Gamesters Handbook* by Brandes and Phillips. [4]

The theoretical base must provide a link between the three previous concepts. It can be extremely difficult for students and social workers to be specific about the theoretical bases from which they work. This often reflects a more general difficulty with which the social work profession struggles, in terms of accepted theories and the desire to be eclectic. Thus statements about the theoretical base of a particular piece of groupwork may appear trite and over-simple, or on the other hand may be so complex as to be almost unfathomable, and unrelated to the purpose of the group.

In examining the four elements of this basic framework with students, I am able to make some assessment of the degree of knowledge and experience that they hold. This will determine whether further direct teaching may be necessary, or reference to particular books, or some other action on my part.

Acquiring Groupwork Skills

By this time, students are often feeling more confident and enthusiastic about the possibilities of groupwork, but have to decide on a project for themselves. There is no overall Unit groupwork project into which students can slot, nor do we run open-ended groups in which they can be absorbed. If students are to have a complete work experience, then they must be involved in the planning, execution, ending and evaluation stages. Therefore the groups are short-term, with fixed membership and time limited in nature. I encourage co-working wherever possible for a variety of reasons, not least the support and sharing that this can provide. Students therefore have the opportunity to try out their ideas, to test out need, and to put theories into action. This can be an exciting opportunity for those with confidence and enthusiasm, or a more daunting task for those who are uncertain of their abilities.

I have found it valuable to explore this area of choosing a project and a co-worker within a group supervision session. At the same time, I introduce the student group to a model of social skills training and personal problem solving which has been developed by Priestley, McGuire et al. [5]

I take the four elements of the theory:

(a) Assessment
(b) Objective setting
(c) Learning
(d) Evaluation

and devise a group session around the problem of choosing a group. I introduce the group to the various assessment methods, and test one or two out with the group. For example, ranking the following list of client groupings in order of preference of working with them:

Fostering/adoption
Physically handicapped
Mentally handicapped
Mentally ill
Adolescents
One-parent families
Marital work
The elderly
Multi-problem families
Ethnic minorities
Non-accidental injury
Administration/organisation
Case recording/report writing
Office duty

When the exercise is completed they discuss with each other their preferences, working for a compatibility of workers in relation to their interests.

The second stage of objective setting establishes a profile of the problem areas, and looks at the steps toward solving the problem. Again I introduce the group to some of the techniques used in the process, and will explain one or two which relate to the problem of choosing a group project. For example, each member is asked to define the problem in terms of what? who? where? when? why? and how?

One of the central concerns for students at this stage is the issue of co-working. Finding a co-worker, choosing and being chosen, or not being chosen, can create great anxiety. The notion of co-working, the suitability of people to work together, and leadership skills can be introduced at the third stage, i.e. learning. Through the use of games and exercises, the group begins to explore the elements of co-operation, the taking and relinquishing of leadership, which is one of the core factors in co-working. A variety of exercises exist. Those I have found useful at this stage include asking the group to divide into pairs, and giving each pair one felt-tip pen and a sheet of paper. Holding the pen together, and without speaking or any other verbal communication, each pair has five minutes to draw their dream house. Occasional snapped pens can result. At the end of five minutes each pair is invited to discuss what happened – how they experienced the exercise – and I try to help each to see how they resolved conflict, i.e. by domination, giving up, tit-for-tat. This exercise is invariably enjoyed by all, as well as being effective.

The balance of power between two workers can be demonstrated by a mirror exercise, particularly when used in conjunction with video playback, so that students can see themselves as well as using feedback from others. The group is divided into pairs. The first pair face each other, and I nominate one to lead the first part of the exercise. His partner has to mirror everything that the leader does for sixty seconds. Then they change roles, and repeat the exercise for another sixty seconds. The third phase involves no designated leader or follower. Each can choose to 'mirror' his partner or not, or initiate an action himself for sixty seconds. The negotiation of power/leadership will vary with each pair, and workers find the comments from others and feedback from the video interesting. This exercise will show:

(a)   people who prefer leading and/or initiating;
(b)   people who prefer to respond rather than lead;
(c)   the   eagerness/reluctance   to   accept/relinquish leadership.

Again there is no perfect relationship, but students can learn their preferred styles of working, or areas for development if a better balance is to be achieved. It will also show those rare workers who are unable to work with anyone else.

Another basic skill group leaders require is the ability to communicate clearly, and to listen carefully. Again this skill can be developed within the learning stage of social skills training. I introduce communicator/receiver games. Pairs sit back-to-back, and one designated communicator has an envelope containing the pattern of a shape, and the six pieces that make up that shape. His partner, the receiver, has an envelope containing only six pieces, without the overall pattern. The communicator has to instruct the receiver verbally how to put the pieces together to make the shape, without using gestures, turning round, or telling him what the overall shape is. The receiver may not speak or gesticulate. I usually allow 8 – 10 minutes, then the receiver and the communicator discuss what happened. It is useful to point out that receivers will often disregard the instructions if they think they know best. It is important to change roles, so that each in the pair has the opportunity to communicate and to receive.

Here are examples of the shapes that can be used:

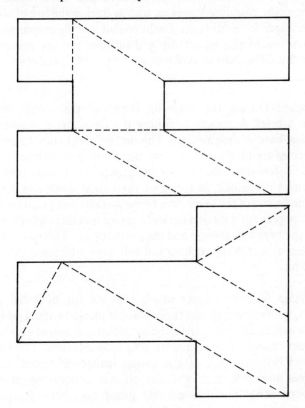

The fourth stage of evaluation is briefly introduced although it is somewhat premature in terms of the group's task of choosing a group. Evaluation forms which social skills training groups have devised can be shared and discussed. Finally I usually ask each worker in turn for a statement about the whole session. This has the value of allowing each student to make something about the session explicit to others. It makes useful feedback for me, although I always take part, and feed back to the group some brief comments about what I think has occurred, what I have valued and learnt.

Supervision of Groupwork Practice

If the group sessions have worked well, I usually find that the students choose co-workers and possible areas of interest. From this stage onwards, supervision usually takes the form of a three-way dialogue with the co-workers, based on more traditional lines. The central goal is to enable workers to increase their levels of skill and knowledge. Supervision sessions are arranged on a regular basis throughout the planning stages as well as during the life of a group, and afterwards for evaluation. I believe that it is the responsibility of the supervisor to give leadership and substance to the sessions, and that this should be done in as objective, democratic, and responsible a way as possible.

Preparation. During the planning stages of the group, workers produce a brief document outlining the aims, type, methods and theoretical base of their project. The timing, frequency and duration of the group are planned, to suit workers' needs as well as to ensure the most successful outcome for the group. They must plan something which is realistic in terms of their total work commitments. When the timing of the sessions is being worked out, I also encourage workers to plan for a session between group meetings where they can discuss the previous session and the one to come. This has to be seen as an integral part of co-working and will cause additional stress if not allowed for.

Membership selection causes much concern for potential group-workers, who often feel that there is some magic formula which will ensure a successful group. As soon as potential members are sought, the group changes from being an idea into a reality. The commitment and responsibility of the group leaders is tested out, and sometimes group leaders will put off this process by protracted discussions about possible suitable group members. Despite this observation, it is important to discuss such variables as open or closed membership, appropriate size, whether age, sex, race, intelligence, communication skills, personality characteristics, problem homogeneity are important, and if so, to what degree? Other important issues which have to be decided are: who will interview prospective members, and how will this be done? what sort of initial contract will be negotiated with members? By 'contract', I mean the demands made by group leaders on members, and the promise of services offered to members by leaders, as well as any rules made at the onset about the group, for example 'no violence'. This can be summed up as the contractual rights and the duties of all parties. There are some agencies which operate 'compulsory attendance' groups, although at FSU the overall values have been based on voluntarism and democratic participation.

Liaison. In setting up most group projects a great deal of liaison is required, not only from the agency within which leaders work, but from other interested agencies and institutions (including families). It can be a crucial factor in running a successful group. One should never take the co-operation of colleagues for granted. They can appear unhelpful, obstructive, defensive or simply uninterested. On the other hand, group leaders can be seen as high flyers in a department, attracting dislike, resentment and jealousy. They can be seen as having a good time at work at everyone else's expense, 'Out all day on an IT project instead of being duty social worker in the office'; 'He always did like playing football instead of working'. Any attempt at intervention which is unusual or out of the ordinary can attract unfavourable comments. Often group leaders' motives are challenged, or the more cynical can play the 'We've seen it all before, and it doesn't work' game.

I have in a simulation exercise for social work students recreated an area team meeting in an imaginary department, the item for discussion being a group project proposal outlined by two social workers. Not only does the exercise show the number of negative reactions that can arise from new proposals, but it allows students to understand the anxieties particular to the different roles of social worker, senior, team leader, area director, etc.

Good liaison is vital for necessary co-operation, and demands clear thinking from the group leaders at the outset of the project. If the project is presented in a half-hearted and muddled way, it is more than likely to fail at the outset. Prospective group workers should always take into consideration their knowledge of organisational and structural behaviour. The elements of decision making within organisations, such as who makes what decisions, who needs to be consulted and informed, have to be recognised if the project is not to be sabotaged.

In my experience, social workers are much better at working with informal structures and can overlook the formal decision-making structures with which they have to deal.

Recording. The style of recording can often be worked out in the planning stages. Recording has to satisfy several requirements. First the needs of the agency, particularly in relation to aspects of accountability, should be established. Also, the needs of 'significant others' have to be considered, for example, social workers or teachers who may have referred group members and may wish for feedback. The balance between feedback, recording and confidentiality has to be worked out with all parties before the beginning of the group. Recording can be vital for evaluating the progress of the group, and assessing the skills of the group leaders. In this respect, recording is an essential tool of supervision.

Once the need for recording has been established, then the style of recording can be considered. For example, in group therapy it may be that the interaction between group members is of central importance; and if so, the use of an 'interaction chronogram' developed by Murray Cox [6] will be useful. A broad-based system of check lists and rating scales can be found in Douglas [3] and these have been considered to be of great value by workers at the Unit.

Co-workers. Throughout the planning stages of the group, the supervisor should be concerned with the development of rapport between the co-workers. This will be demonstrated by the effectiveness of their joint efforts in the planning of the group. The supervisor may set tasks or exercises specifically designed to increase rapport between co-workers, sharing and exploring their worst fears of the group, sharing weaknesses they fear will be exposed in the group. Many of these ideas have been borrowed from those used by David Wilmot in training courses in the FSU in-service training programme.

Supervision of Groups in Progress
During the life of the group supervision focuses on the progress of the group towards its defined aims, and the developing knowledge and experience of the group leaders. In order to work towards these

aims in supervision, it is necessary for the supervisor to acknowledge and share with the group leaders some theoretical framework of group process which helps to bring together theory and practice.

This is no easy objective, for the literature on group process is varied and complex. First, our theoretical concepts about group behaviour derive from social psychology, criminology, sociology, learning theory, psychoanalytic theory and humanistic psychology among others. Second, classification of groupwork depends on which variables are used, for example the setting, the clientele, the aims.

There have been various attempts to establish models of group-work practice, notably by Papell and Rothman, Roberts and Northern, [7] and Allen Brown. [9] I find these typologies useful, but in my view none of them have advanced the concept of the developmental stages of group process to the degree achieved by the Boston University School of Social Work, and outlined by Garland, Jones and Kolodny. [10]

Their central concern was to develop a model which explained what happened between the beginnings and endings in the life of a group. They based their model on three central assumptions:

(a)   That closeness is a central theme in the development of social work groups.
(b)   That frames of reference used by members for perception and behaviour in groups can be identified.
(c)   These frames of reference change as the nature of the group experience changes.

The five stages of development or growth of a social work group are seen as:

1. Pre-affiliation — characterised by approach and avoidance behaviour, where the frame of reference is society.
2. Power and control — characterised by problems of status, rank-ing, communication and intra-group control dynamics. The frame of reference is one of transition.
3. Intimacy — here feelings are brought more into the open, the group develops a system of relationships oriented to a more family-like model. The frame of reference becomes the family.
4. Differentiation — group cohesion now allows members to accept one another as distinct individuals, the group is seen as a unique experience. The frame of reference becomes internal, i.e. the group.

5. Separation — the group reacts to ending in a variety of ways, for example denial, regression, recapitulation, evaluation etc. The frame of reference is the group experience, and may be taken into new situations.

This brief outline of a model for group process can form a basis in supervision for linking theory with practice in groupwork. For a detailed exposition and synthesis of groupwork theory, I would refer readers to a recent publication by Tom Douglas. [11]

In selecting an appropriate frame of reference, it may be useful to locate the proposed group on a continuum thus:

Highly cohesive, task-oriented group, involving some submission of individual needs	⟷	Loose-knit grouping of individuals each meeting own needs with little concern for others, or whether group really becomes a group.

A broad framework of aims in supervision includes not only the ability to develop theoretical constructs, and incorporate them into practice, but the elements of 'cognitive structuring' which can include the refining of past learning, and the integration of research findings into practice. Two other central aims of supervision are:

(a)   The development and evaluation of practice skills, such as observation, accurate recording, communicating, 'therapeutic responsiveness' and other inter-personal skills; and

(b)   personal and emotional development, gaining an understanding of the dynamics of one's own behaviour and personality, and the effect on clients or group members.

The major techniques of supervision can be outlined as follows:

1. Use of recording.
2. The didactic method.
3. Direct observation.
4. Direct help.
5. The supervisory conference.

1. The use of recording has already been outlined earlier, and I find it invaluable for developing groupworkers' skills at observing and understanding group process.

2. The didactic approach to supervision which emphasises learning through specific cases is often valued highly by students. A variety of techniques within this approach can be used, for example role-playing, simulations, paper and pencil exercises. I have devised such an exercise to help co-workers to evaluate practice skills and personal styles of leadership for themselves and for each other. Each worker completes the following questionnaire:

(a) List three skills you feel you possess as a group leader.
(b) List three skills your co-worker possesses as a group leader.
(c) List one aspect of your co-worker which caused you difficulty.
(d) List three things you have learnt as a group leader.
(e) List one quality you would like to possess as a group leader.
(f) What have you appreciated most about the group?
(g) What have you disliked most about the group?

I also define three skills that I feel each worker possesses as a group leader, and in the three-way sharing and discussion a great deal of valuable feedback is acquired.

3. Direct observation is seldom used in the supervision of social groupwork, although the use of observers in T groups is a recognised practice. I have not found direct observation to be appropriate in Family Service Units, although the use of video recording allows an element of this.

4. Similarly the use of direct help has been minimal. The apprenticeship model appears to work best in agencies employing continuous group therapy programmes, whereby the worker can progress from the apprentice role towards the master role.

5. The supervisory conference has been described by Miller [12] as 'the keystone of the arch of supervision'. It is within this structure that the aspects of teaching and learning take place, that interpretation and evaluation are discussed, and the development of group leadership and co-leadership skills are encouraged.

Although I have referred to co-leadership at several stages during this chapter, it may be useful to share at this point the basic framework that I find most useful. This is the distinction between (a) task-oriented leadership roles and (b) group maintenance leadership roles.

(a) Task oriented skills involve — achieving group goals, giving and seeking information and opinion, initiating, summarising, reality-testing etc.

(b) Group maintenance skills involve — feelings, relationships, participation, evaluating emotional climate, observing processes, resolving conflict, building trust etc.

These skills can be evaluated and plotted on a two-dimensional grid according to answers to an exercise devised by Johnson and Johnson. [13]

I also divide skills into general and specific. General skills include the ability to create and maintain an effective group designed to achieve its task. Specific skills may include the ability to lead games and exercises, the ability to use psychodrama or generate group discussion. A study on the factors determining successful co-working by Paulson, Burroughs and Gelb [14] isolated three crucial areas:

(a) Theoretical orientation of workers.
(b) Ways of identifying and handling problems in terms of style and skill of workers.
(c) The quality and quantity of participation of workers.

The supervisor needs to be aware of the importance of these areas if successful co-working is to be achieved.

I have attempted in this chapter to describe not only my practice as a groupwork supervisor, but to outline the theoretical concepts and frameworks that I have found useful. Much of what I have written now seems to me to be obvious and common sense. However, I am aware that, like myself, many social workers with responsibility for groupwork were trained in casework, and often feel insecure in their groupwork knowledge base. For them, I hope that some of the ideas set out in this chapter will prove helpful.

References

1. Quoted (without original source) in A. Kadustun, 'Games People Play in Supervision'. *Social Work*, Vol 13, No. 3, July 1968.

2. P. Parsloe, N. McCaughan and K. McDougall (eds.) *Groupwork, a Guide for Teachers and Practitioners*. National Institute for Social Work Papers No. 7, 1977.

3. T. Douglas, *Groupwork Practice*. Tavistock, 1976.

4. D. Brandes and H. Phillips. *Gamester's Handbook*. Hutchinson, 1978.

5. P. Priestley, J. McGuire et al, '*Social Skills and Personal Problem Solving*. Tavistock, 1978.

6. M. Cox, 'The Group Therapy Interaction Chronogram'. *British Journal of Social Work*, Vol. 3, No. 12, 1973.

7. R. W. Roberts and H. Northen, *Theories of Social Work with Groups*. Columbia University Press, New York, 1976.

8. C. P. Papell and B. Rothman, 'Social Groupwork Models, Possession and Heritage.' *Journal for Education in Social Work*, Vol. 2, No. 2, 1966.

9. A. Brown, *Groupwork*. Heinemann Educational, 1979.

10. J. A. Garland, H. E. Jones and R. L. Kolodny, 'A model for Stages of Development in Social Work Groups,' in S. Bernstein (ed) *Explorations in Groupwork*. Boston University School of Social Work, 1965.

11. T. Douglas, *Group Processes in Social Work*. John Wiley, 1979.

12. S. Miller, 'Distinctive Characteristics of Supervision in Groupwork'. *Social Work*, Vol. 5, No. 1, 1960.

13. Johnson and Johnson, *Joining together Group Theory and Group Skills*. Prentice Hall, 1975.

14. I. Paulsen, J. C. Burroughs and C. B. Gelb, *International Journal of Group Psychotherapy*, 1976.

5. Support and Supervision of Volunteers

Pam Wood

Introduction

Leicester FSU has a fairly lengthy history of use and involvement of volunteers in family work. However, in order to give a firsthand account of support and supervision of volunteers, the period under consideration can only be since my appointment at Leicester FSU in June 1978. In doing that, I am not denying the very real and positive contribution that volunteers had made to Unit services until that point in time. The way in which the Unit works with volunteers is a fairly rare experience, about which very little has been documented. Exceptions are the Barnardos/Channel project [1] and the Guild of Service project pioneered by Beth Humphries [2], with which there are broad similarities. However, that is not to say that there are not other similar projects of which I am unaware, and indeed a number of other Family Service Units are experimenting with the use of volunteers at this present moment.

When I was appointed it was the first time in the Leicester Unit that a specific post had been created to carry responsibility for volunteers, albeit half-time; and marked a recognition that the use of volunteers should be an integral part of the services that the Unit offered, rather than the responsibility for a volunteer programme 'tacked on to' another post within the Unit. It was recognised that the post should be occupied by a qualified and experienced social worker, in order to facilitate integration in the staff team, which is not the situation with similar posts in most social services departments. The period under consideration is between June 1978 and March 1980 which was a period of great stability in the staff group at the Unit, a situation likely to enhance the success of a new project.

In what follows, I shall attempt to outline how we set about defining the role of volunteers within the agency, including the aims of the project and the assumptions about the use of volunteers, and go on to illustrate the sort of tasks that this definition generated for volunteers. I shall point out the limitations that this had and the consequences for the programme. This ultimately led to a revision of aims and objectives and a redefinition of the role of volunteers within the agency. Within this role definition I shall outline some of the work that volunteers are now engaged upon.

Having set the context, I shall then look at the concept of support, which I see as an umbrella term encompassing a range of activities such as selection, training, supervision and integration; and attempt to draw out characteristics that would appear to be common to all of these, such as accountability, responsibility, personal growth of the volunteer, dissemination of knowledge, acquisition of skills; and an examination and modification of attitudes and how in a broad sense they are applicable to the support offered at Leicester FSU.

Third, I shall describe in more detail the growth of the volunteer programme at Leicester FSU, giving particular attention to how support and supervision are offered to volunteers and how these have developed. Finally, I shall give some consideration to the future of the volunteer programme at Leicester FSU and the ways in which I would like to see it develop, which include a more systematic way of evaluating the service, development of the support of groups of volunteers within the the Unit, and the implications that the increased use of volunteers has for social work training.

Why Volunteers?

Before one considers the role that volunteers play in any agency, perhaps one needs some clarity about the definition of a volunteer. It seems to me that the notion of a volunteer being 'someone who undertakes a job for no monetary gain and of his own volition', (3) although a very broad definition, is a satisfactory starting point. In practice this has meant that we have considered and used a wide range of people, have been involved in taking a number of risks, but have also had at our disposal a wide variety of different skills and personal qualities.

Before employing volunteers, and also as a continuing process, the most fundamental thing an organisation needs to do is to work out the role that volunteers are going to play, otherwise support and supervision have no context within which to operate. The consequences of not doing it can be disastrous and could lead to the breakdown of the whole project. My initial task at Leicester was to gain some knowledge of the staff group and their attitudes to volunteers, and to work out with them the role of volunteers in the agency. A number of discussions ensued from which we felt some clarity emerged. However, it was no mean task and with hindsight, although we put a fair amount of time and effort into this, I do not believe we achieved a satisfactory definition, the consequences of which I will illustrate later. We have with experience achieved more clarity, and no doubt this will be a continuing exercise, but it would be unrealistic to expect that one could achieve clarity in any other way than by experience.

However, the broad assumptions and aims of the volunteer programme at that time were as follows: The Unit had a broad commitment in theory to the use of volunteers and the development of a volunteer programme, and this was reflected in the attitudes of the individual members of staff. There was an agreement that volunteers played a complementary role to the professionals, one of the roles decribed by Holme and Maizels [4] in their survey of volunteer involvement. The main elements of this role appear to be that volunteers have specific skills and experiences that professionals do not have; they also have personal qualities, such as warmth, friendship, spontaneity and creativity which the professional role often limits. Therefore, in their involvement with families they have things to offer which are complementary to that which the social worker is offering. The idea of the volunteer having specific skills to offer was recognised in the early days of the programme, whilst the idea of important personal qualities beyond the limits of the professional role was recognised much later. There was also a recognition that some tasks with family situations were rightly and properly undertaken by a social worker, e.g. marital work, whereas there were other tasks which could be done equally well if not better by a volunteer, because of the very qualities recognised above, e.g. learning to shop more economically. Whilst there was a recognition that volunteers were not second-rate social workers, and therefore were equals, there was also a recognition that what they had to offer was different from the social work task. Consequently, they needed to be accountable for the work they were doing and this clearly implied supervision.

There was also some clarity about the role that they were not expected to play. We did not see them in any way as cheap labour. We did not necessarily expect that they would give the professionals more time, particularly in the early days of training, placement and supervision; although in the long term, we hoped that professionals might be released from some tasks in order to take on tasks which required professional skills. Most of all, we did not see the volunteer as a 'filler of gaps' that the professionals were unable to attend to, due to lack of resources. This seems even more pertinent in the present economic and political climate, and something which I feel very strongly that we should guard against as an agency. It is interesting that this seems also to have been a philosophy that Beth Humphries [2] adopted in her project.

Initially, these ideas led to a role for volunteers within the agency that was very specific, task-centred, time-limited and contract-based. This fitted the way that the professionals within the Unit were working at the time. It does seem to me that the role that volunteers assume has to be in tune with the ethos of the agency at any one time. This meant that volunteers were engaged on work such as baby-sitting, assisting families to organise their shopping more economically, arranging holidays, linking individuals with groups in their local community. The consequence of this approach was that the professionals were not generating enough of this type of work to keep the volunteers fully occupied. Understandably, this was frustrating for the volunteers; they felt let down and under-used and we were in danger of losing some of them. I felt that the volunteer programme was somewhat isolated from the other activities of the agency, that it was not well integrated, and that I was constantly attempting to express the needs and problems of each group to the other, but unable to create any real change.

A reappraisal of the whole programme was required and in the summer of 1979 I set about doing that. A working party was set up drawing representatives from the various areas of the Unit, e.g. case-work, groupwork, student unit, secretarial and administrative. We attempted to look at the reasons why insufficient work had been generated and to reassess the role of volunteers within the agency. These ideas were then presented to the volunteers for comment. The major reasons for the lack of work appeared to be as follows: although there was a commitment in theory from everyone to the programme, individuals had failed to examine their workload closely enough to discover and release tasks for volunteers. There was also a move in the Unit at the time towards a more structured form of family therapy, where the power base for the work was retained in the social worker, thus making it difficult for them to involve a volunteer other than on fairly mundane tasks. There was also a lack of imagination on the part of the agency to think about new and innovative ways of involving volunteers, and a failure on my part to look for work outside the agency. In addition, the specific task-centred work that most of the volunteers were involved in left some of them feeling that initiative and spontaneity was unwelcome, and therefore they were stifled and unfulfilled.

The findings of the working party brought forth a recommitment from the Unit to the volunteer programme and the idea of a more extensive role for volunteers, with which the volunteer group were in total agreement. The extension of the role included more work in the area of general support and befriending of families, with the qualification that this must be purposeful and time-limited. However, it allowed for more initiative and creativity. There would still be opportunities for task-centred work with families as part of continuing intervention. Tasks generated by the structured family therapy approach would still be available but a volunteer would normally take on such a task in addition to other work. Project work for volunteers was also a possibility, but ideas for this would need to be generated. Volunteers had not been involved in the groupwork programme at all until the reappraisal, and there was some indication of possibilities in this area. Volunteers could also continue to be involved in one-off practical tasks, as an addition to their normal work.

The implications of this broader role for volunteers were at least threefold. The initial training programme would need to more broad-based than in the past, to prepare people for a wider variety of work. Therefore, the social worker supervising the volunteer would have to offer him more training in order to prepare him for any specific task. Then there would seem to be a need for regular assessment and evaluation of the volunteer programme, in order to try and prevent this situation arising again.

After such a lengthy exposition of why volunteers are involved at Leicester FSU, you may be left wondering what on earth they actually did; and a few examples of the areas of work outlined above might now be appropriate. Joyce, a volunteer in her late fifties has been offering a befriending role to Carol, a single parent in her late twenties with two young children. Carol was adopted when she was a baby and had recently traced her natural parents through new provisions in the 1975 Children's Act. She had arranged to visit them at Christmas. Her social worker was leaving FSU before Christmas and had been working with Carol on behavioural problems that she had with the children. It was felt likely that the experience of meeting her natural parents would be very stressful for Carol, and that she would like the opportunity to prepare for it and to evaluate it on her return. Joyce was engaged to befriend Carol and to help her through this fairly difficult period. At the same time, Joyce was involved in babysitting for a family for a fixed number of sessions, where the social worker is working on a structural family therapy model, and is encouraging the parents to go out together. Another volunteer Jane, a single woman in her mid-twenties, has been involved in some task-centred work with Sue, a woman in her mid-twenties with four children who had recently separated from her husband. Sue was quite depressed and wished to start to redecorate her home, but lacked the motivation to do it. Jane visited for a fixed period of time to encourage and help Sue decorate two of the rooms in her house.

Two newly trained volunteers were engaged in some project work in the summer. We had a number of single parents who were wanting to take their children on holiday, but none of them particularly wanted to go alone. Jane and Margaret, the two volunteers, were asked to explore alternative forms of holiday for a group of these parents to go together. They also had to cost the holiday and book the most appropriate one, visit the families who were interested and arrange for them to come along to group planning meetings. From time to time, the Unit has a lot of one-off practical tasks to be completed. Several of our volunteers have been involved in helping make up and deliver Christmas hampers, help at the Christmas toy-shop, transport families to hospital or on holiday etc.

Why Supervision and Support?
Support is a very global term, perhaps best defined by Redman [5]:

> Support means whatever is needed to assist the individual in developing his or her own task as volunteer. That may mean offering opportunities for the volunteer's development as a person, or helping him or her through a crisis, or providing him or her with information, or any combination of these and other types of support.

Support is an umbrella term made up of several elements such as selection, training, supervision, and integration of the volunteer in the team. These in turn also have specific characteristics, making the nature of support an extremely complex notion. At Leicester FSU these various elements tend to merge and overlap, so that training includes elements of selection and supervision includes ongoing training; and the format of training and supervision encourages integration. To consider any one in isolation becomes an academic exercise. However, each of us can probably think back to a time in our life when we felt unsupported, and in recalling that experience, can probably remember some of the feelings of ignorance, helplessness, frustration, isolation and uncertainty that went along with this. Consequently, we would all probably agree that support is extremely important, yet in the study undertaken by Holme and Maizels [4] they discovered how few volunteers receive adequate support.

Although support is made up of various components, perhaps it is possible to pull out some characteristics, common to them all, which illustrate its nature and importance; and then attempt to demonstrate in the following section how these have worked out in practice and demonstrate the areas of overlap.

The twin concepts of accountability and responsibility would appear to be major components of support. As an agency we have a responsibility to the clients, to the volunteer and to the community for the quality of the work that we do, and therefore a responsibility to ensure that our work is effective. We do not only have a responsibility for the standard of the work that a volunteer does, but we also need to assist him/her in developing and improving their skills. This may be by giving advice and guidance, it may be by offering opportunities to practise new skills, it may be by providing opportunities for the most appropriate approach. However, although we operate from the assumption that most people have something to offer, taken to its logical conclusion responsibility means that we may decide not to accept some people. We acknowledge that the sort of work that we ask volunteers to do can impose stresses and strains upon them and therefore we look for people with particular qualities. We seek those who are reasonably mature and have a fair amount of stability in their lives at the present moment. Within that, we are prepared to take risks and would consider ex-clients as volunteers and people who have experienced a fair number of personal problems themselves – because we believe people can grow and have something to offer from their own experiences. I believe that we can take that sort of risk, precisely because we offer good and regular supervision. The unspoken qualities that we look for seem to be such things as reliability, warmth, sensitivity, tolerance, flexibility and an ability to make good relationships.

Of course, whether you consider that an individual has those qualities must partly be a value-judgment, and as such, always open to question. Having accepted a volunteer we also have the responsibility to place him in the right situation, to match his skills and capabilities with the task required to be done, both for his protection and that of the client. However, in practice our ability to match volunteers and tasks is extremly crude, and sometimes it has become a matter of merely finding a job for a volunteer. Leicester FSU have also made a policy decision that families, groups and projects where a volunteer is involved are the responsibility of the Unit, chiefly through the volunteer organiser, but with support from colleagues.

In return, the volunteer must be accountable to the agency,

through his supervisor, for the work that he is doing. This involves recording work, and attending training sessions, supervision sessions and volunteers' meetings. It also entails sticking within the boundaries of the task, which are set by the social worker and the volunteer organiser in the initial contract. It is sometimes difficult to preserve this without stifling initiative and one is always struggling to achieve a balance, so that both the client's and the volunteers' interests can best be served. A policy statement made in writing to the volunteers sums this up by saying 'responsibility and accountability is *not* to frustrate individuals in their endeavours to help, but to give security and protection to clients, volunteers and the agency'.

The question of confidentiality also falls into this realm. It has been clearly stated by the Unit that information is confidential to the agency and not the individual and therefore the volunteer has a responsibility to pass on any information which she feels is important to the ongoing work. At the same time, the volunteer is given sufficient information about a family to enable her to do her task and she is expected not to pass that information on to other people. As an agency, we feel fairly clear that if an individual cannot operate within these constraints of accountability and responsibility, then she should cease to be a volunteer. One could continue to cite other examples of the importance of responsibility and accountability. It is however sufficient to acknowledge them as important components of support and to recognise that they are part of the supervisory process, to be taken into account by the social worker responsible for the family or group, or by the volunteer organiser.

Another aspect of support is the personal growth of an individual as a volunteer. We recognise that she is not only doing a job for the agency but should be getting personal satisfaction for herself and hopefully developing new skills. The supervisor has a responsibility to ensure that the volunteer's needs are being met, and that she is being helped to realise her potential. A number of volunteers have come to the agency looking for opportunities to test out whether they wish to enter the caring professions. One needs to recognise with them that this is an acceptable motivation, and help them to recognise strengths and weaknesses and hopefully give them opportunities to work at the latter. One volunteer has moved into social work, another to community work and one to psychiatric nursing. Part of my role for all three of these has been to offer some counselling on career possibilities. Some volunteers have started with fairly simple tasks and as they have gained confidence and skill have moved to more complex ones. I feel that part of my support role is to offer guidance and encouragement in this sort of development. Some volunteers require less support as they develop, others require more because they undertake more complex work and engage in more self-examination. Some volunteers require a lot of support for even simple tasks. Thus, to some extent the support offered has to be tailored both to the needs of the individual and to the task involved.

Another function of the support process is to offer knowledge to the volunteer: knowledge about the agency for which they are working and its function, knowledge about the job they are to undertake and about the resources necessary to do it, and about the limitations of the job. Support should also offer an opportunity for volunteers to become aware of their skills and personal qualities and how these could be best used in each particular situation, and also an opportunity to develop and acquire new skills that a job might require. Another aspect of support should be the opportunity to explore attitudes; both the attitudes of the volunteer to particular client groups, problems and situations, and the attitudes of other significant people – for instance, the attitudes of their own family, the community and other agencies. If attitudes are totally incompatible with the purpose of the agency, this might be a reason for rejecting a volunteer; if less extreme it might be an opportunity for changing or modifying attitudes. Thus support and selection may have an educative process.

From time to time volunteers may have personal problems in their own lives and part of the support process might be offering the volunteer an opportunity to discuss his problems. However, I do not believe in caseworking the volunteer and would only see this as being appropriate if it were something the volunteer raised himself, or where his problems were obviously affecting the work he was doing as a volunteer. Ultimately this may mean ceasing to be a volunteer, as it has done on one occasion at Leicester FSU, if the problems appear insurmountable.

Somewhere within the support process there should also be an opportunity for volunteers to communicate with the professionals, to offer their comments and criticisms on things which they have experienced as volunteers, on the services which they see the agency offering and to contribute to the policy making of the agency. This has only happened quite recently at Leicester FSU, since volunteers have gained more confidence and become more organised. It can only happen where the paths of communication between volunteers and professionals are open, and where the volunteer programme is seen as an integral part of the agency. Linked with this must be the preparation of colleagues for the coming and use of volunteers – thus develops the educative role of the volunteer organiser with his colleagues. Once this process has begun, the involvement of colleagues in all aspects of the volunteer programme seems to be the best way of encouraging them to use volunteers, integrating volunteers into the agency and opening up the channels of communication.

A further aspect of support is adequate preparation of the client. There must be an acceptance of the introduction of a volunteer, and a clear understanding of the task that the volunteer is to perform, with its boundaries and limitations explained. The best way of achieving this at present seems to be a joint meeting between the client, social worker and volunteer, where a clear contract about the involvement is made and the expectations on all sides are clearly understood.

In offering support to a volunteer, in all its various forms and combinations and with all its differing combinations, it is also important that the volunteer organiser receives adequate and appropriate support. I have been fortunate to have good supervision myself, and have worked in a very cohesive and supportive staff group. I have also had the opportunity to practise new skills and to attend training courses. Yet even so, there have been times when I have felt isolated and unsupported, particularly at the time when I had insufficient work for the newly trained volunteers. This leads me once again to emphasise how important it is to work out very clearly in the agency the role that volunteers are going to play, before embarking on a volunteer programme.

The Practice of Volunteer Support

At present there are eight active volunteers and four currently on an induction course. The project is not particularly large, but the agency decided that because of its size and the nature of its work we could only actively support about fifteen volunteers. I spent quite a considerable time familiarising myself with volunteers, getting to know the formal and informal support networks in Leicester, e.g. Volunteer Organisers Forum, and setting up communication with possible referring agents, e.g. Voluntary Workers Bureau and social services. The former proved to be a major source of referral for volunteers and over the period in question we have built up a very clear understanding about the sort of people we are prepared to consider. Thus, a fair amount of selection takes place even at this early stage. Working out the role of volunteers within the agency was the parallel exercise going on at this time.

There were four volunteers from previous days who still had some contact with the Unit, although only two of them were working with families. I ran a short refresher course for these volunteers, mainly to familiarise them with changes in the approach to family work that had taken place in the Unit. The two who were not working then took on some short-term task-centred work with families. (The content and format of the course will be discussed later, when considering induction training generally.) I was then able to begin to think about recruiting, training and placing new volunteers.

Most people who apply to be volunteers at the Unit are referred by the Voluntary Workers Bureau, who in turn use the local paper and radio to recruit on our behalf. A few people apply after having heard about us from other sources, and one or two have been passed on by social services. I offer each person who makes an enquiry a preliminary interview, when I give information about the agency, the sort of work volunteers might be asked to do, and the training and selection process. I then ask them to think about the situation and make a formal application if they wish to continue. Quite a lot of people select themselves out at that stage, and I have a deliberate policy not to pursue people from whom I do not hear. When I receive the formal application I take up references, from two people who know them well and could comment on their suitability for the sort of work we would ask them to undertake. Having received that information I have a further interview with the individual, based on data given on the application form.

We discuss employment, family circumstances, interests, previous experience, motivation etc. Few people drop out at this stage, although it was necessary to ask one individual to withdraw because it was felt that he would not cope with the stresses of the work he might be asked to do.

The next stage is to ask the volunteer to join a six-session induction course, and no volunteer is used until they have completed the course. The object of the course is to enable volunteers to know more about the reality of being a volunteer at FSU and therefore decide whether it is appropriate for them or not. It also gives myself and the rest of the staff, because they are all involved in the training process, an opportunity to make decisions about the suitability of the individuals, and to gain some idea on both sides about potential placements. So far, I have trained thirteen new volunteers in three groups; the objective is to keep the group fairly small, but to operate with a minimum of three persons. We aim to run courses about three times per year, so that no individual has to wait too long for a course. Of the thirteen people involved, two dropped out, one was counselled out, and the four on the current course are still unknown quantities. In the initial courses, despite spending a lot of time working them out, we were unclear about the objectives of training. The content of the sessions was therefore ad hoc, offering what we felt would be 'good' for the volunteers. The sessions did not always link, the volunteers were unclear about what was happening, and at the end of the training had little clarity about what was expected of them. However, since our reappraisal we have clarified the objectives of the course as being selection and self-selection of volunteers, and matching to appropriate tasks. We have also developed a better framework for the course, offering the volunteers knowledge, the opportunity to acquire skills, the exploration of their own attitudes and considering the elements of support and supervision. Understandably, the objectives of training are bound to require experience in order to gain clarity, and will continue to change as the programme develops and grows.

The emphasis of the course is on learning from one's own experience and ideas, rather than by more formal teaching methods. The methods used include role plays, games, exercises, simulations, talks, handouts etc. Some of the older volunteers found these methods rather difficult to cope with initially, and would have preferred a more formal teaching style, but appear to have warmed to them towards the end of the sessions. I also offer an individual interview in the middle of the course, to discuss any problems with the learning process and any queries the volunteer feels unable to settle in the group, and this has proved useful for dealing with all sorts of fears, anxieties and misconceptions. There is also a final interview at the end of the course, where I attempt to offer some feedback to the individual about strengths and weaknesses; we assess what she has gained from the course and together decide the most appropriate work for her. The volunteer may decide at this stage to withdraw or may need to be counselled out, which has happened in only one case. Where I am uncertain at this stage, we have agreed that the volunteer should have a further interview with the Unit Organiser. When the volunteer is accepted (s)he is given a certificate stating that (s)he is an accredited volunteer at Leicester FSU. Volunteers also receive a written copy of their assessment and this is used as a basis from which to think about their future development. Towards the end of the course, issues such as confidentiality, accountability, responsibility and supervision are discussed, thus leading gently into the next stage of support.

When a social worker has a task for a volunteer, they would discuss it with me and together we would decide who might be the most suitable person to undertake it. This would depend on who was available for work at that time, who had the capabilities to undertake the task, based both on my assessment and the social worker's knowledge of the volunteers. The two of us would then meet the volunteer to discuss the task and the volunteer would make a decision about it. In practice volunteers rarely refuse work and one needs constantly to question why that is so. Individual supervision for the work would be offered to the volunteer by the social worker involved, if he was continuing to work with the family. If not, I would normally supervise the volunteer, and in practice I tend to supervise more volunteers than anyone else because social workers generally involve a volunteer at the end of their own work. In theory, new family referrals which are allocated straight to a volunteer would also be supervised by me, but in practice this has not happened. Practical one-off tasks might be supervised by the administrative staff, and volunteers in groups by the groupworker.

The most important thing is that each volunteer has a link person in the Unit for each piece of work that they do, and would have regular supervision sessions with him and could also contact him in-between. The nature and frequency of those sessions depend on the needs of the volunteer and the requirements of the task. There is also an understanding that volunteers supervised by another worker can come back to me for discussions if they are experiencing difficulties, which we may then need to discuss further with the social worker. The individual supervision session would appear to incorporate most of the elements of support described earlier, such as accountability, responsibility, opportunities for individual development, sharing of knowledge, development of skills, and exploration of attitudes. Volunteers are expected to produce a summary of their work on a monthly basis, but are not particularly good at this; this could be a useful topic for group supervision sessions. On only one occasion have I needed to use supervision to explore with a volunteer the desirability of her continuing, and finally to counsel her out.

Apart from individual supervision, we also have a volunteers group, which meets monthly. This has a training function, in that half the session is devoted to speakers, discussions, films, or role plays, whilst the other half is administrative. It provides an opportunity to keep the volunteers in touch with the developments in the Unit and developments in the volunteer programme, and lately has encouraged them to be involved in decision making about both. It also provides an opportunity for volunteers to meet each other and in that way give each other mutual support. I see the group as belonging to the volunteers, and therefore wanted them to decide how the time could best be used. In the early days they found it very difficult to generate ideas, and it is only over the last eight months that they have begun to do this, partly as they have grown in confidence and also after I shared with them my concern about the volunteer programme, and asked them to contribute to the findings of the working party. They have recently run two of the sessions without me and whilst this has shattered my theories of indispensability, it has demonstrated an increasing independence. However, the group is still small in number; about half the volunteers attend regularly and feel frustrated by those who do not, because they feel that if they were stronger they could be a more powerful group within the agency. There is a hope at the moment that the new volunteers will join them and swell their potential.

However, despite their smallness, they have generated a number of good ideas. They felt very strongly that they wanted to become more involved in the Unit, particularly in the decision-making process, and also wanted to get to know staff better; as they felt isolated and on the periphery of the organisation and therefore unsupported. These feelings were conveyed by me to the staff group and the volunteers now have a representative in the Unit meeting. She has a responsibility to feed back to the group what is happening in the Unit, and to put the volunteers' point of view on issues being discussed. So far, this opportunity has not been used as well as it might, but it is something on which we need to continue to work.

The volunteers have also suggested that they invite some of the staff group to their monthly meeting to examine their views on particular political and economic issues, because in representing FSU they feel they want to know more about the attitudes and values of the agency on whose behalf they work. There is also a desire for more informal staff/volunteer contact, and we have had two fairly successful social events, a beer and skittles evening and a cheese and wine and games evening. These various activities have served to open up the channels of communication between the professionals and the volunteers, and create a better working relationship.

The practice of two-way communication seems to me to be a very important part of the support process. As volunteers and professionals have more contact, it becomes more difficult for the professionals to ignore volunteers as an important section of the total Unit, and more likey that they will continually reappraise their workload for tasks for volunteers to do. The welcoming, informal atmosphere in the Unit also plays a large part in volunteers feeling part of the Unit and then being able to make a positive contribution to its development. It seems to me that if the Unit staff, from the cleaner to the Unit Organiser, do not make time and space for volunteers, then it is unlikely that volunteers will enjoy their work and feel adequately supported.

Finally there was a decision by the working party to reconvene from time to time, to look at the progress of the volunteer programme. This has taken place once so far, to discuss my ideas for the most recent induction course. It seems extremely important to have a vehicle for evaluation in order to produce an effective volunteer programme, and to ensure that volunteers have the most appropriate support and supervision. Whether this working party is the most useful tool for this purpose remains to be tested out.

The Future of the Volunteer Programme

One of the most important things to ensure for the future would be some measure of the effectiveness of the volunteer programme. It seems to me that one of the major objectives of support and supervision is to encourage effectiveness. By giving to the volunteer, one increases the chances that the client will receive a good service. Over the years, the effectiveness of social work as a profession has been questioned time and time again, and as yet no-one has developed a very satisfactory scientific way of measuring the effectiveness of the service. Therefore, for Leicester FSU to produce a scientific way of measuring the effectiveness of its volunteer programme is somewhat unrealistic. However, there may be some ways in which we can acquire some feedback about the service offered, and make an assessment of its effectiveness, albeit somewhat subjectively.

Evaluation has not been done in a systematic way up to this point. For instance, we already have a working party which could be used as a vehicle to collate and evaluate feedback, and no doubt the volunteers group could also participate. Feedback from individual volunteers about training, supervision and their work with clients would be a starting point. Volunteers have objectives for their involvement and should be able to assess how far these objectives have been met. Feedback from social workers, observing volunteers working with families where they still have involvement, is of great value. Feedback from the families themselves would also be very useful information; we could say the intervention has been effective if they feel that they have been helped and have valued the contact with the volunteer. This might seem to be a very cumbersome exercise, but in the end, if we are to justify scarce resources, the work which we do must be seen to be effective. Therefore, a regular reappraisal of the role of volunteers at Leicester FSU by the working party is important and information about effectiveness is necessary in order to do this properly.

Another area for support for future development might be the training and support of groups of volunteers within the community. At the present moment we recruit volunteers from the four corners of the city, and place them with families anywhere in Leicester. Whilst I would want this area of work to continue, I can also see real value in developing, training and supporting local community care groups, which might eventually become self-supporting. Offering a city-wide service to families might restrict this development and perhaps it would be more appropriate if we worked a 'patch system'. Whether it would be possible for the Unit to offer this in addition to the programme already operating, within the limits of a half-time post, is also questionable – but still a development worth thinking about.

Whilst over the last few months there has been a move for the volunteers to become more integrated within the Unit, I would want to see this continuing to develop. Hopefully, the volunteers groups will grow and will then become a more powerful group for action. I would like to see them becoming a more critical force within the Unit – but acknowledge that this is a slow process. Whilst they now have a representative at Unit meetings, perhaps they should also be present in other meetings and discussion groups that take place in the Unit, e.g. referral meetings or group supervision. I would also like current volunteers to be more involved in selection, training and supervision of other volunteers. The idea of volunteers not only assisting in the induction course, as they do at present, but also being part of the final decision making about who is accepted and for what sort of tasks, is frightening but exciting. The idea of volunteers supervising or consulting each other is also appealing, although one would have to work out the lines of accountability and responsibility.

Finally, the effective use of volunteers depends on social workers being educated to the potential of volunteers and the role that they can play within the social work process. This has implications for both CQSW courses and in-service training of social workers in their daily setting. It seems to me that agencies who are using volunteers, and have not only made an attempt to work out the role that they can play, but also have some experience of testing that out in practice, have a responsibility to share their knowledge and experience with other social workers. To that end, we have considered the possibility of offering a one-day workshop to social workers in Leicester; but maybe this needs to be part of a plan in conjunction with other social workers who also have experience of using volunteers.

References

1. *Barnardo's Channel Voluntary Family Counsellors, 1973 – 77.* Barnardo Social Work Papers No. 3, 1977.

2. B. Humphries, *Only Connect.* Guild of Service, 1976.

3. 'The Involvement of Volunteers in Family Casework — a Case Study.' *A Case in Point,* No. 5, The Volunteer Centre, 1977.

4. A. Holme and J. Maizels, *Social Workers and Volunteers.* Allen and Unwin/BASW, 1978.

5. W. Redman, *Working with Volunteers: No. 1 Support.* The Volunteer Centre, 1977.

Conclusions

In the preceding chapters we have drawn on the experience of three units to give a range of examples of supervision in action. We would not claim that the examples given comprise a complete picture of the full range of supervisory techniques for social workers, nor even within FSU itself. We have instead attempted to use a descriptive form which gives some detailed examples of methods of work and their consequences for social work teams. Our purpose in this has been to describe work in such a way that others may take from it what seems to them relevant for their own setting and practice.

It may seem foolhardy to have included in this book theoretical frameworks as widely diverging as psychodynamic social work, systems theory and the unitary approach. For many, these would appear to be opposite camps in social work practice. No apology is made for this, for what we hope to have shown is that despite differing theoretical bases, common themes for supervision and team management emerge.

The first, and perhaps the most important of these themes is the priority which should be given to staff supervision if effective work is to take place with a difficult client group. The chapters by Janet West, Pam Donnellan and Pam Wood provide valuable examples of the practice skills which need to be acquired by workers, students and volunteers alike, in order to gain confidence and develop an effective service to clients. The chapter by Gemma Blech highlights the importance of supervision not only in supporting workers who are undertaking emotionally demanding work in high-risk family situations, but in enabling those workers to achieve change, for if the worker becomes stuck in the complexity and the turmoil of the families' lives, then 'burn out' becomes a certainty.

The second theme that is common to all this work is the inter-relationship between supervision and team management. This is made most explicit in the chapter by David Horn and Rosemary Clews of the East Birmingham Unit. The implications of attempting to put into practice the theories of the unitary approach affected not only staff supervision and individuals' professional development. It also affected the whole management structure of the Unit, the organisation of team meetings, and communication within the team, and with other agencies and the local community. Similarly it can be seen that the supervision of groupwork, students and volunteers in the Leicester Unit has implications for the management and communication in the team as a whole, and each draws considerably on the techniques used for the others. Communication and team structure are also seen as crucial in the work of the Queens Park Unit.

A third theme, which is made with force by Gemma Blech, is the commitment and participation of all members of the team to its way of working. The recruitment and appointment of all staff in FSU is a process which is given time and care, and in which all members of a staff team normally share. We regard it as essential that any new member of staff should have an opportunity to know in some detail the beliefs and the theories that underlie the work, and to meet the colleagues who form the team. Equally, the team needs the opportunity to explore the commitment, ideas, skills and compatibility of a new team member. In all Family Service Units, participation of all team members in decision making goes alongside a shared responsibility for the standards of work of the whole unit. This may make for lengthy decision making at times, and care needs to be taken that meetings do not outweigh direct work with clients. However, these problems are far outweighed by the resulting increase in strong teamwork, and individual commitment and responsibility.

The final point that should be made is the ultimate objective of all this work. For any social work agency, good supervision, support and development of its staff, and strong teamwork, important though they may be, are only the means to the most important objective – the best and most effective service to its clients.